Blumenfeld's

Phonics for Success

The Road to High Literacy Made Easy

"The Red Book that can conquer Illiteracy"

Samuel L. Blumenfeld

We now live and work in a global information-based economy where knowledge is king. *Phonics for Success* gives every child super easy access to that knowledge

Workbook & Instruction Manual

Samuel L. Blumenfeld Literacy Foundation
Windham, New Hampshire

Blumenfeld's **Alpha-Phonics©**
Workbook

New Revised Edition, October 1997
New Printing, October 2005
Phonics for Success Version, February 2014
ISBN number 978-1-4951-4421-9

Phonics for Success
48 Pine Street, Suite J1
Waltham, MA 02453
781-647-0205
Cell: 781-354-2040

Samuel L. Blumenfeld Literacy Foundation
7 Blueberry Road
Windham, New Hampshire 03087-1143
603-434-9695

Copyright © 1983, 1997, 2005, 2014 by Samuel L. Blumenfeld. All rights reserved. No part of this book may be reproduced in any form whatsoever without written permission from the publisher, except by a reviewer who may quote brief passages in connection with a review or article.

Printed in the United States of America

CONTENTS

Preface	v
The Alphabet 　Pre-reading Alphabet Exercises	viii
Student's Lessons	3
Order of Lessons	133
English Alphabetic System Common Spelling Forms	136
Introducing Cursive 　Cursive Alphabet	139
About the Author	142
Instruction Manual	1-38

Dedicated to

Bob and Joy Sweet
Dear Friends and Founders of the
National Right to Read Foundation

PREFACE

Blumenfeld's Phonics for Success was created to provide parents, teachers and tutors with a sensible, logical, easy-to-use system for teaching reading. It is an intensive phonics instruction program based on the author's many years of research and experience in the reading instruction field. It answers the need for a practical instruction program that anyone who wants to teach reading can learn to use with a minimum of training.

Phonics for Success is designed to help the learning child achieve high literacy so that he or she will be able to take advantage of all the career opportunities offered by our information-based economy. The no-nonsense *Workbook* is absent of pictures because pictures are a distraction and do not teach anyone to read. Parents need no special training to be able to teach this program. All they have to do is simply follow the instructions in the Instruction Manual.

The Workbook teaches our entire alphabetic system. First, the alphabet, then the short vowels and consonants, the consonant digraphs, followed by the consonant blends, and finally the long vowels in their variety of spellings and our other vowels.

This program can be used to teach reading to beginners of all ages, older students in need of remediation, illiterate adults or those who wish to improve their reading skills, dyslexics, the learning disabled, and non-English speakers who wish to learn to read English and improve their pronunciation.

It can also be used as a supplement to any other reading program being used in the classroom. Its systematic approach to teaching basic phonetic skills makes it particularly valuable to programs that lack such instruction.

The program's step-by-step lessons in large, easy-to-read print make it suitable for both direct one-on-one tutoring and regular classroom use. Parents may also want to obtain the Little Readers which were written to give children the exciting experience of reading their first book. By the time they have completed the program they will be able to read just about anything.

All of the lesson pages were carefully designed to eliminate distraction and help the learner focus his or her attention on the work at hand. The program, as a whole, is flexible enough so that any parent, teacher, or tutor can adapt it to his or her own teaching style or situation.

If you have never taught reading before in this sensible, systematic way, you will be pleasantly surprised by the results.

— Samuel L. Blumenfeld

The Alphabet
and
Pre-reading Alphabet Exercises

Aa Bb Cc Dd

Ee Ff Gg

Hh Ii Jj Kk

Ll Mm Nn Oo Pp

Qq Rr Ss

Tt Uu Vv

Ww

Xx Yy Zz

A B C D
E F G
H I J K
L M N O P
Q R S
T U V
W
X Y Z

Capital Letters
(Also known as upper case letters)

a b c d
e f g
h i j k
l m n o p
q r s
t u v
w
x y z

Small Letters
(Also known as lower case letters)

Pre-reading Alphabet Exercises

A	B	C	a	b	c
B	B	C	b	b	c
C	A	B	c	a	b
B	C	A	b	c	a
C	B	A	c	b	a
C	C	A	c	c	a
C	A	C	c	a	c
C	B	C	c	b	c
D	E	F	d	e	f
E	F	D	e	f	d
F	E	D	f	e	d
F	E	F	f	e	f
F	D	E	f	d	e
F	F	D	f	f	d
E	E	F	e	e	f
F	D	F	f	d	f

x

G	H	I	g	h	i
G	G	I	g	g	i
I	G	H	i	g	h
H	H	I	h	h	i
H	I	G	h	i	g
G	G	I	g	g	i
G	I	H	g	i	h
H	G	G	h	g	g
J	K	L	j	k	l
J	J	K	j	j	k
L	L	J	l	l	j
L	K	L	l	k	l
L	J	K	l	j	k
K	J	J	k	j	j
J	K	J	j	k	j
K	L	J	k	l	j

M	N	O	m	n	o
M	O	M	m	o	m
O	N	N	o	n	n
N	O	M	n	o	m
N	M	O	n	m	o
O	M	O	o	m	o
O	O	N	o	o	n
O	N	M	o	n	m
P	Q	R	p	q	r
R	P	Q	r	p	q
Q	Q	P	q	q	p
Q	P	Q	q	p	q
R	R	P	r	r	p
R	P	R	r	p	r
P	R	P	p	r	p
R	P	P	r	p	p

S	T	U		s	t	u
S	U	S		s	u	s
T	S	U		t	s	u
T	U	T		t	u	t
T	S	S		t	s	s
S	T	S		s	t	s
U	T	S		u	t	s
U	U	S		u	u	s

V	W	X	Y	Z		v	w	x	y	z
Z	V	W	X	X		z	v	w	x	x
W	W	Y	Z	X		w	w	y	z	x
W	Y	W	Y	Z		w	y	w	y	z
X	Y	Z	V	V		x	y	z	v	v
Y	Z	Y	X	V		y	z	y	x	v
Z	X	Y	X	W		z	x	y	x	w
W	Z	X	Y	V		w	z	x	y	v

Blumenfeld's
Phonics for Success
Student's Lessons

Lesson 1

a → m → am

a → n → an

a → s → as

a → t → at

a → x → ax

Aa Mm Nn Ss Tt Xx

Lesson 2

S → am → Sam

m → an → man

h → as → has

s → at → sat

t → ax → tax

Hh

Lesson 3

am	an	as	at	ax
Sam	man	has	sat	tax

Sam sat.
Sam has an ax.

Lesson 4

a → d ⟶ ad
d → ad ⟶ dad
w → ax ⟶ wax
D → an ⟶ Dan

Dan sat.
Dad has wax.

Dd Ww

Lesson 5

ad	am	an	as	at	ax
had	ham	man	has	hat	tax
dad	dam	Dan	was	sat	wax
sad	Sam	tan		mat	Max
Tad					
mad					

ad	dad	had	mad	sad	Tad
am	dam	ham	man	sat	tan
an	Dan	has	mat	Sam	tax
as		hat	Max		
at					
ax					

was
wax

Lesson 6

Dad sat.
Max had ham.
Dan was tan.
Was Sam tan?
Has Dad an ax?
Dad has an ax.
Dan has wax.
Sam was sad.
Was Max mad?
Tad was tan.

Lesson 7

an → d   → and
h → and   → hand
l → and   → land
s → and   → sand

Dan and Dad had land and sand.

Dan and Sam
Max and Tad
tax and wax
land and sand

Ll

Lesson 8

Ll

A → l → Al
H → al → Hal
S → al → Sal

Bb

b → ad → bad
b → an → ban
b → and → band
b → at → bat

Cc

c → ab → cab
c → ad → cad
C → al → Cal
c → at → cat
c → an → can

Lesson 8

(Continued)

Gg

g → ab ──────────→ gab
g → ad ──────────→ gad
g → ag ──────────→ gag
g → al ──────────→ gal
g → as ──────────→ gas

Ff	Jj	Ll	Nn
fad	jam	lab	nab
fan	Jan	lad	nag
fat	jab	lag	Nat
fax	jag		

Lesson 9

Pp	Rr	Tt
pad	rag	tab
pal	ram	Tab
Pam	ran	Tad
pan	rap	tag
pat	rat	tan
Pat		tap
		tax

Vv	Ww	Yy	Zz
Val	wag	yak	zag
van	wax	yam	zap
vat	was	yap	

Kk

Lesson 10

ab	ad	ag	ak	Al
cab	bad	bag	yak	Cal
dab	cad	gag		gal
gab	dad	jag		Hal
jab	fad	lag		pal
lab	gad	nag		Sal
nab	had	rag		Val
tab	lad	sag		
	mad	tag		
	pad	wag		
	sad	zag		
	Tad			

Lesson 10

(Continued)

am	an	ap	as
cam	ban	cap	gas
dam	can	gap	has
ham	Dan	lap	[was]
jam	fan	map	bass
Pam	Jan	nap	lass
ram	man	rap	pass
Sam	pan	sap	
yam	ran	tap	
	tan	yap	
	van	zap	

13

Lesson 10

(Continued)

at	ax	az	and
bat	fax	Yaz	band
cat	lax	jazz	hand
fat	Max		land
hat	tax		sand
mat			
Nat			
pat			
rat			
sat			
vat			

Lesson 11

ck

ack	Mack	tack
back	pack	yack
hack	rack	Zack
Jack	sack	
lack		

qu

quack

Lesson 12

a

a cat	a pal
a hat	a bag
a bat	a rag
a cap	a cab
a pan	a map

Qu qu

15

Lesson 13

Al can bat.
Jack has a sack.
Pam has a fat cat.
Val has jam.
Jan has a cap.
Cal has a hat.
Yaz can bat.
Mack has a jazz band.
Yaz can yack.
Jack has a back-pack.
Can Yaz bat?

Lesson 14

ab	bab	cab	dab
ac	bac	cac	dac
ack	back	cack	dack
ad	bad	cad	dad
af	baf	caf	daf
ag	bag	cag	dag
al	bal	cal	dal
am	bam	cam	dam
an	ban	can	dan
ap	bap	cap	dap
as	bas	cas	das
at	bat	cat	dat
av	bav	cav	dav
ax	bax	cax	dax
az	baz	caz	daz

Lesson 14

(Continued)

fab	gab	hab	jab
fac	gac	hac	jac
fack	gack	hack	jack
fad	gad	had	jad
faf	gaf	haf	jaf
fag	gag	hag	jag
fal	gal	hal	jal
fam	gam	ham	jam
fan	gan	han	jan
fap	gap	hap	jap
fas	gas	has	jas
fat	gat	hat	jat
fav	gav	hav	jav
fax	gax	hax	jax
faz	gaz	haz	jaz

Lesson 14

(Continued)

kab	lab	mab	nab
kac	lac	mac	nac
kack	lack	mack	nack
kad	lad	mad	nad
kaf	laf	maf	naf
kag	lag	mag	nag
kal	lal	mal	nal
kam	lam	mam	nam
kan	lan	man	nan
kap	lap	map	nap
kas	las	mas	nas
kat	lat	mat	nat
kav	lav	mav	nav
kax	lax	max	nax
kaz	laz	maz	naz

Lesson 14

(Continued)

pab	rab	sab	tab
pac	rac	sac	tac
pack	rack	sack	tack
pad	rad	sad	tad
paf	raf	saf	taf
pag	rag	sag	tag
pal	ral	sal	tal
pam	ram	sam	tam
pan	ran	san	tan
pap	rap	sap	tap
pas	ras	sas	tas
pat	rat	sat	tat
pav	rav	sav	tav
pax	rax	sax	tax
paz	raz	saz	taz

Lesson 14

(Continued)

vab	wab	yab	zab
vac	wac	yac	zac
vack	wack	yack	zack
vad	--	yad	zad
vaf	waf	yaf	zaf
vag	wag	yag	zag
val	wal	yal	zal
vam	wam	yam	zam
van	--	yan	zan
vap	wap	yap	zap
vas	--	yas	zas
vat	--	yat	zat
vav	wav	yav	zav
vax	wax	yax	zax
vaz	waz	yaz	zaz

Lesson 15

a	e	i	o	u
bad	bed	bid	Bob	bud
bag	beg	big	bog	bug
hat	hen	hit	hot	hut
pan	pen	pin	pop	pun
sat	set	sit	sock	sun
Nat	net	nit	not	nut
ban	Ben	bin	bop	bun
bat	bet	bit	box	but
pat	pet	pit	pot	pup
pack	peck	pick	pock	puck
dad	deck	did	dock	dud
tack	Ted	tick	tock	tuck
hack	hen	hick	hock	huck
ham	hem	him	hop	hum
Dan	den	din	Don	duck
lag	leg	lip	log	lug
lack	let	lick	lock	luck
ran	red	rib	rob	rub

Lesson 16

Short e

eb	eck	Ed	eff	egg	ell
Deb	beck	bed	Jeff	beg	bell
web	deck	fed		keg	cell
	neck	led		leg	dell
	peck	Ned		Meg	fell
		red		peg	jell
		Ted			sell
		wed			tell
					well
					yell

> cell
> sell

Lesson 16

(Continued)

em	en	end	ep	et	ex
gem	Ben	bend	hep	bet	Rex
hem	den	fend	pep	get	Tex
	fen	lend	rep	jet	vex
	hen	mend		let	
	Jen	rend		met	
	Ken	send	es	net	
	Len	tend	yes	pet	
	men	wend	Bess	set	
	pen		less	vet	
	ten		mess	wet	
	yen			yet	

Lesson 17

Bess fed Jack an egg.
Let Jeff tell Ben.
Can Rex tell Pam?
Deb had an egg.
Dad let Ken get wet.
Deb has a red pen.
Send Len an ax.
Lend Jen a pet.
Ben has a jet.
Rex fell.
Tell Bess yes.
Deb can yell.
Ted has a cat as a pet.
Get Jeff a keg.
Tex and Len set a net.
Bess has less.
Ten men met.

Lesson 18

beb	ceb	deb	feb	heb
bec	cec	dec	fec	hec
beck	ceck	deck	feck	heck
bed	ced	ded	fed	hed
bef	cef	def	fef	hef
beg	ceg	deg	feg	heg
bel	cel	del	fel	hel
bem	cem	dem	fem	hem
ben	cen	den	fen	hen
bep	cep	dep	fep	hep
bes	ces	des	fes	hes
bet	cet	det	fet	het
bev	cev	dev	fev	hev
bex	cex	dex	fex	hex
bez	cez	dez	fez	hez

Lesson 18

(Continued)

jeb	keb	leb	meb	neb
jec	kec	lec	mec	nec
jeck	keck	leck	meck	neck
jed	ked	led	med	ned
jef	kef	lef	mef	nef
jeg	keg	leg	meg	neg
jel	kel	lel	mel	nel
jem	kem	lem	mem	nem
jen	ken	len	men	nen
jep	kep	lep	mep	nep
jes	kes	les	mes	nes
jet	ket	let	met	net
jev	kev	lev	mev	nev
jex	kex	lex	mex	nex
jez	kez	lez	mez	nez

Lesson 18

(Continued)

peb	queb	reb	seb	teb
pec	quec	rec	sec	tec
peck	queck	reck	seck	teck
ped	qued	red	sed	ted
pef	quef	ref	sef	tef
peg	queg	reg	seg	teg
pel	quel	rel	sel	tel
pem	quem	rem	sem	tem
pen	quen	ren	sen	ten
pep	quep	rep	sep	tep
pes	ques	res	ses	tes
pet	quet	ret	set	tet
pev	quev	rev	sev	tev
pex	quex	rex	sex	tex
pez	quez	rez	sez	tez

Lesson 18
(Continued)

veb	web	yeb	zeb
vec	wec	yec	zec
veck	weck	yeck	zeck
ved	wed	yed	zed
vef	wef	yef	zef
veg	weg	yeg	zeg
vel	wel	yel	zel
vem	wem	yem	zem
ven	wen	yen	zen
vep	wep	yep	zep
ves	wes	yes	zes
vet	wet	yet	zet
vev	wev	yev	zev
vex	wex	yex	zex
vez	wez	yez	zez

Lesson 19

Short i

ib	ick	id	if	ig
bib	Dick	bid	Jiff	big
fib	hick	did	miff	dig
jib	kick	hid	tiff	fig
rib	lick	kid		gig
	Mick	lid		jig
	Nick	mid		pig
	pick	rid		rig
	quick	Sid		wig
	Rick			zig
	sick			
	tick			
	wick			

zig-zag

Lesson 19

(Continued)

ill	im	in	ip	is
Bill	dim	bin	dip	his
bill	him	fin	hip	sis
dill	Jim	kin	kip	
fill	Kim	pin	Kip	iss
gill	rim	sin	lip	hiss
hill	Tim	tin	nip	kiss
Jill	vim	win	pip	miss
mill			quip	
pill			rip	
quill			sip	
rill			tip	
sill			zip	
till				
will				

Lesson 19

(Continued)

it	ix	iz		**Ph**
bit	fix	Liz	quick	Phil
fit	mix	quiz	quill	Philip
hit	nix	fizz	quip	
kit	six		quit	
lit			quiz	
pit				
quit				
sit				
wit				

Ph ph

Lesson 20

Quick, Rick, fix it.

Tim bit his lip.

Nick is sick.

Nick will get well.

Will Bill tell Jill?

Sid will miss his pet pig.

His pig is big.

Jim is big.

His hat fit him well.

Phil hid his hat.

Jack hid his ham in his hat.

Liz was sick and was fed in bed.

Mix it, fix it, and quit it.

Will Bill win?

Yes, Bill will win.

Is Jill ill?

Yes, Jill is ill.

Lesson 21

th

th → at	→	that
th → an	→	than
th → e	→	the
th → em	→	them
th → en	→	then
th → is	→	this
th → in	→	thin
th → ick	→	thick
ba → th	→	bath
ma → th	→	math
pa → th	→	path
Be → th	→	Beth
Se → th	→	Seth
wi → th	→	with

Lesson 22

That man has a cat.
The cat is a big cat.
The cat is a thin cat.
This is his cat.
This is Beth.
Tell them that Rex is at bat.
The cat is in the bag.
Did Beth tell them that the cat
   is in the bag?
Rick hid the bag with the cat.
The cat ran.
Let the cat dig in the sand.
The pig ran with the cat.
Dick ran with the bag in his hand.
Phil was with Beth and Seth.
Then Beth and Seth ran with the hen.
Quick, get the thick net.

Lesson 23

Short <u>o</u>

ob	ock	od	of	og	oll
Bob	dock	cod	off	cog	doll
cob	hock	mod		dog	loll
job	lock	nod		fog	
gob	mock	rod		hog	
mob	pock	sod		jog	
rob	rock	Todd		log	
sob	sock				

tick-tock

36

Lesson 23

(Continued)

om	on	op	ot	ox
mom	Don	cop	cot	box
Tom	Ron	hop	dot	fox
	son	mop	got	lox
	ton	pop	hot	pox
	won	top	jot	
			lot	
			not	
			pot	
			rot	
			tot	

pom-pom
Red Sox

Lesson 24

The quick fox got on top of the box.
The red hen fell in the bath and
 got wet.
The Red Sox will win.
Yaz will win.
Tom is the son of Jack.
The dog ran with the cat.
The pot got hot.
Is the dog in the box?
The dog is not in the box.
The dog is on top of the box.
Bob and Don sat on the dock.
Tell Mom that Bob has the mop.
That fox is in the big tin box.
That box has a lock on it.
Quick, lock the box.
But the fox ran.

Lesson 25

[s]

cat → s ⟶ cats
dog → s ⟶ dogs
pet → s ⟶ pets
wig → s ⟶ wigs
pig → s ⟶ pigs
pill → s ⟶ pills
pot → s ⟶ pots
pan → s ⟶ pans
hand → s ⟶ hands

[es]

kiss → es ⟶ kisses
box → es ⟶ boxes
tax → es ⟶ taxes
fox → es ⟶ foxes

['s]

Don → 's ⟶ Don's hat
Bob → 's ⟶ Bob's dog
Jack → 's ⟶ Jack's pet
Jill → 's ⟶ Jill's cat

Lesson 26

The man has ten cats and six dogs.
Jill has six hens.
Jim's pet pig is big.
Don kisses his mom.
Pam's cat is fat.
Pat has ten pins.
Jack has six boxes of eggs.
Mom has ten pots and six pans.
Rex's hat is red.
The dog ran with the foxes.
Val's dog was in the pen.

Lesson 27

Short u

ub	ud	ug	ull	um	un
cub	bud	bug	cull	gum	bun
dub	dud	dug	dull	hum	fun
hub	mud	hug	gull	mum	gun
pub		jug	hull	sum	pun
rub		lug	bull		run
sub		mug	full		sun
tub		rug	pull		
		tug			

up	us	ut	ux	uzz
cup	bus	but	lux	buzz
pup	Gus	cut		fuzz
	pus	hut		
	fuss	mutt		
	muss	nut		
		put		

Lesson 28

The dog dug in the mud and had fun.
Tom's dad put the pup in the tub.
Can Jack pull the big log up the hill?
Jack and Jill ran up the hill.
The red jug is full.
The dog got mud on the rug.
Bud's dog fell in the tub.
Gus put the mug on the rug.
Rick hugs his pup.
The sun was up at six.
The tub is full of mud.
The bug dug in the rug.
A big bull is in the pen.
Val put the mud in the tub.

Lesson 28a

bad	bed	did	bob	dud
dad	deb	bid	bod	dub
dab	ded	bib	dod	bud
bab	beb	dib	dob	bub

Lesson 29

sh

a→sh

ash	mesh	dish	gosh	gush
bash		fish	Josh	hush
cash		wish	posh	mush
dash				rush
gash				**bush**
lash				**push**
mash				
rash				
sash				
wash				

---

sh→ag

shag	shed	shin	shock	shun
sham	shell	ship	shop	shut
shall			shot	
shack				

43

Lesson 30

ch

ch ▸ ap

chap   check   chick   chop   chuck
chat   chess   chill   chug
               chin   chum
               chip

ri ▸ ch

rich   much
       such

Lesson 31

wh

wh ▸ en

when   which
whack   whim
                  whiff
                  whip
what   whiz

Lesson 32

cash	fish	chess
what	chop	shock
ship	shop	chuck
rich	much	shack
shut	rash	chug
dish	which	what
chill	shell	chin
wish	when	check
rush	chick	which
when	such	ash
dash	shed	shot
mush	shun	chap
chum	chip	whip
mash	shag	hush
chug	whim	whack

Lesson 33

Don had fish and chips.
Which dish is Dad's?
Which dish has the fish in it?
This dish is full of chips.
Pam sat on the deck of the ship.
Don has a chill. Bud has a rash.
Rick has cash and is rich.
Bud is his chum.
His chin is thin.
He hid the dish of fish in the shed.
When will Jim shut the shop?
The shop will shut when it is six.
Chuck is in the shack.
Dad has a chess set.
Chuck will wash the ship.
Pam will pull the dog off the ship.
Did Bess check the shack?
Bess did check the shack.

Lesson 34

I am   I have
you are   you have
he is   he has
she is   she has
we are   we have
they are   they have

I was   I had
you were   you had
he was   he had
she was   she had
we were   we had
they were   they had

Lesson 35

I have a cat.
She has a dog.
We have a cat and a dog.
They have six pets.
You have a pet pig.
Are you sick?
No, I am well.
She put the pup on the bed.
The pets were in the tub.
They were in the hut.
He had a rash.
Did you get sick?
No, I did not get sick.
Did she win?
Yes, she won.

Lesson 36

is not → isn't
can not → can't
has not → hasn't
it is → it's
let us → let's
did not → didn't

Lesson 37

Is Bill sad?   Bill isn't sad.
Is this Peg's dog?   No, this isn't Peg's dog.
Is it Jill's dog?   Yes, it's Jill's dog.
Has Peg a cat?   Peg hasn't a cat.
Can they run?   They can't run.
Did Jill run?   Jill didn't run.
Let's not jog.   Let's run.

Lesson 38

hot-dog	hotdog
box-top	boxtop
zig-zag	zigzag
cat-nip	catnip
tick-et	ticket
hel-met	helmet
vel-vet	velvet
tom-cat	tomcat
gal-lop	gallop
les-son	lesson
nap-kin	napkin
tid-bit	tidbit
hab-it	habit
rap-id	rapid
gal-lon	gallon
can-did	candid
bas-ket	basket
bon-net	bonnet

Lesson 38
(Continued)

ton-ic	tonic
mag-ic	magic
un-fit	unfit
gob-lin	goblin
rob-in	robin
chap-el	chapel
pic-nic	picnic
kid-nap	kidnap
lin-en	linen
vis-it	visit
rab-bit	rabbit
nit-wit	nitwit
viv-id	vivid
civ-il	civil
Nix-on	Nixon
len-til	lentil
pen-cil	pencil

Lesson 38

(Continued)

egg-nog	eggnog
com-et	comet
pup-pet	puppet
up-set	upset
lock-et	locket
mim-ic	mimic
pub-lic	public
sun-tan	suntan
sud-den	sudden
hat-box	hatbox
sun-set	sunset
hat-rack	hatrack
bash-ful	bashful
den-tal	dental
un-til	until
vom-it	vomit
hus-band	husband
wag-on	wagon

Lesson 38
(Continued)

ex-it	exit
Phil-ip	Philip
riv-et	rivet
with-in	within
Cal-vin	Calvin
tab-let	tablet
pack-et	packet
rock-et	rocket
sock-et	socket
van-ish	vanish
pan-el	panel
Ja-pan	Japan
ras-cal	rascal
cac-tus	cactus
cam-el	camel
Kev-in	Kevin
Kar-en	Karen
rib-bon	ribbon

Lesson 38

(Continued)

rad-ish	radish
mas-cot	mascot
com-bat	combat
Pat-rick	Patrick
rel-ish	relish
lem-on	lemon
pock-et	pocket
traf-fic	traffic
bob-cat	bobcat
sig-nal	signal
lim-it	limit
li-quid	liquid
sat-in	satin
tun-nel	tunnel
cab-in	cabin
jack-et	jacket
pad-lock	padlock

Lesson 39

Jill has a picnic basket full of hotdogs and relish.

Philip has a suntan.

Kevin is a rascal.

Karen and Ken will visit dad.

Calvin put the pencil in his jacket pocket.

Bill's mascot is a rabbit.

Don put a red ribbon on his cat.

Mom has a red satin bonnet.

Peg's husband has a wagon.

The camel sat on the cactus.

Pam can mimic a puppet.

Deb has a red velvet sash.

Jim has a gallon of lemon tonic.

Let's visit Patrick's dad.

It was a vivid sunset.

Lesson 40

a *as in* all

Al	all	ball
Cal	call	fall
gal	gall	mall
Hal	hall	tall
pal	pall	wall

Cal's pal Tim is tall.
Did Hal fall?
Cal has the ball.
Cal hit the ball with the bat.
Philip sat on the wall.
His jacket is in the hall.
Call Cal.
Tell Cal that his ball is in the hall.
Is the ball in his jacket pocket?
Yes, it is.

Lesson 41

ng

ang	ing	ong	ung
bang	bing	bong	hung
gang	ding	gong	lung
hang	king	long	rung
pang	ping	song	sung
rang	ring		
sang	sing		
	wing		
	zing		

ding-dong   wing-ding
ping-pong   Hong Kong
sing-song

Deb sang a song.
Ron rang the bell.
The song was sung.
The king can sing.
The gang sang.
Tim is in Hong Kong.

Lesson 41

(Continued)

Wash-ing-ton
Washington

dab	dabbing	ring	ringing
gab	gabbing	sing	singing
rob	robbing	run	running
rub	rubbing	sun	sunning
pack	packing	nap	napping
pick	picking	tap	tapping
lock	locking	chip	chipping
rock	rocking	chop	chopping
bid	bidding	ship	shipping
kid	kidding	shop	shopping
dig	digging	fish	fishing
rig	rigging	wish	wishing
call	calling	wash	washing
fall	falling	rush	rushing
sell	selling	pass	passing
yell	yelling	toss	tossing
chill	chilling	fit	fitting
will	willing	quit	quitting
bang	banging	fix	fixing
hang	hanging	mix	mixing

Lesson 42

Jan is singing a song.
Bill is ringing the bell.
Peg is getting all wet.
Rick is kicking the ball.
The cat is licking his leg.
Bob is calling his dog.
Jack is yelling at Jill.
Pat is packing his bag.
Cal is passing the ball.
Chuck is fixing the shack.
Meg is petting the cat.
Is Mom shopping at the mall?
Dad is chopping with his ax.
Jill is napping on the bed.
Bess is washing her doll.
Philip is dabbing at the sand.
Was Kim digging in the mud?

Lesson 43

nd

and	end	wind	bond	fund
band	bend		fond	
hand	fend		pond	
land	lend			
sand	mend			
wand	rend			
	send			
	tend			

nt

ant	bent	pent	hint	bunt
pant	cent	rent	lint	hunt
rant	dent	sent	mint	punt
want	gent	tent	tint	runt
	Kent	vent		
	lent	went		

Lesson 44

Bill is mending his tent.
Kent went hunting.
Jack went with Kent.
Bob lent Ann his fishing rod.
Ann is fishing at the pond.
Bob wants his rod back.
Bob went to the pond.
Jill is fond of Philip.
Philip sent Jill a bag of mints.
The cat sat on the ant hill.
Beth is running in the wind.
Kent is in the band.
Mom will mend Pam's socks.

Lesson 45

er	→ her
let-ter	letter
bet-ter	better
hunt-er	hunter
lend-er	lender
send-er	sender
but-ter	butter
ten-der	tender
chat-ter	chatter
big-ger	bigger
sum-mer	summer
win-ter	winter
sis-ter	sister

Butter is better.
Ken has a sister.
Her hat is bigger.
Bill sent a letter.
Her dad is a hunter.
Summer is better than winter.

Lesson 46

	nk			**nch**	
bank	ink	honk	ranch	bunch
Hank	kink	bunk	bench	hunch
lank	link	dunk	inch	lunch
rank	mink	hunk	finch	munch
sank	pink	junk	pinch	punch
tank	rink				
yank	sink	**nc**		
	wink	zinc		

Lesson 47

Hank put cash in the bank.
Bob put gas in the tank.
Beth put the dish in the sink.
Bill had a bunch of junk.
Dan sat on a bench.
Dad has a ranch.
Tim had lunch with Bess.
Bev had punch with her lunch.
Pam has the top bunk.

Lesson 48

ct	ft	pt	xt
act	aft	apt	next
fact	raft	kept	text
pact	left	wept	
tact	gift		
duct	lift		
	rift		
	sift		
	loft		
	soft		

Bill got a raft as a gift.
He left his raft at the pond.
The raft is big.
Can Bill lift the raft?
The fact is that he can't.
But Jack and Bill can lift the raft.
Ann got a gift.
Jan will get the next gift.
Can Beth act? Yes, she can.
Liz will sift the sand.

Lesson 49

sk	**sp**		**st**	
ask	asp	cast	pest	list
bask	gasp	fast	test	mist
cask	rasp	last	rest	cost
mask	lisp	mast	vest	lost
task	cusp	past	west	bust
desk		vast	zest	dust
disk		best	chest	gust
risk		jest	quest	just
dusk		lest	fist	must
rusk		nest	gist	rust
whisk				

Jim sat at his desk.
Jill will pass the test.
Beth did her best.
Bill went west.
Bob did his task.
Hank can run fast.
The metal chest was full of rust.

Lesson 50

lb	**ld**	**lf**	**lk**
bulb	held	elf	milk
	meld	self	silk
	weld	golf	bulk
		gulf	hulk
		shelf	sulk

	bald	**calf**	**talk**
		half	walk

Lesson 51

lm	**lp**	**lt**	
elm	help	belt	hilt
helm	kelp	felt	jilt
film	yelp	melt	tilt
	gulp	pelt	wilt
	pulp	welt	quilt

		halt	
		malt	
		salt	

Lesson 52

mp

camp	limp	bump	lump
damp	chimp	dump	pump
lamp	romp	hump	sump
champ	chomp	jump	chump

Lesson 53

tch

catch	itch	etch	botch
hatch	ditch	fetch	notch
latch	hitch	retch	Dutch
match	pitch		hutch
patch	witch		
watch			

Jack has an itch. Dad lit a match.
Dad has a watch. Bess has a lamp.
The cat is in a ditch at the dump.
Can the cat catch the fish?
Bill will pitch his tent at the camp.

Lesson 54

dge		**nge**
badge	dodge	binge
Madge	lodge	singe
edge	budge	tinge
hedge	fudge	lunge
ledge	judge	
wedge	nudge	
ridge	hodge-podge	

The cat sat at the edge of the ledge and did not budge.

Lesson 55

nce		**nse**
dance	mince	dense
chance	since	sense
fence	dunce	tense
hence	once	rinse

The cat sat on the fence.
The fog is dense.

Lesson 56

match	bath	went
milk	jump	half
left	elm	weld
ring	tint	dance
dust	rinse	with
dish	edge	hint
belt	bank	pitch
pest	act	rich
cash	ink	rust
fudge	help	fast
kept	much	test
pink	next	elf
lung	patch	fist
desk	hunt	witch
last	west	fond
lost	sing	send
melt	camp	bend
catch	itch	fence
bulb	gasp	ranch
bench	kept	once

Lesson 57

con-test	contest
sand-wich	sandwich
self-ish	selfish
rub-bish	rubbish
pol-ish	polish
den-tist	dentist
ab-sent	absent
pun-ish	punish
shop-lift	shoplift
af-ter	after
ob-ject	object
dust-pan	dustpan
con-duct	conduct
bath-mat	bathmat
fin-ish	finish
con-sent	consent
chop-stick	chopstick
hodge-podge	hodgepodge

Lesson 58

bl

blab	bled	bliss	bluff
black	blend	blob	blunt
blanch	bless	block	blush
bland	blimp	blond	
blank	blink	blot	
blast	blip	blotch	

br

Brad	brash	brig	broth
brag	brass	brim	Bronx
bran	bred	bring	brunch
branch	brick	brink	brunt
brand	bridge	brisk	brush

Lesson 59

cl

clad	clasp	cling	cloth
clam	class	clip	club
clamp	cleft	clock	cluck
clan	clench	clod	clump
clank	click	clog	clung
clap	cliff	clop	clutch
clash	clinch	clot	

cr

crab	crash	crick	crunch
crack	crass	crimp	crush
craft	crept	crisp	crust
cram	cress	crock	crutch
cramp	crest	crop	crux
crank	crib	cross	

Lesson 60

dr

drab	drank	drift	drop
draft	dredge	drill	drudge
drag	drench	drink	drug
dram	dress	drip	drum

dw

dwell   dwelt

Lesson 61

fl

flab	flax	fling	flub
flack	fleck	flint	fluff
flag	fled	flip	flung
flank	flesh	flock	flunk
flap	flex	flog	flush
flash	flick	flop	
flat	flinch	floss	

Lesson 61

(Continued)

fr

Fran	fret	frost	frill
France	fresh	froth	frisk
Frank	French	from	frizz
Fred	frog		frock

Lesson 62

gl

glad	glint
glance	glitch
gland	glob
glass	glop
glen	glum
glib	glut

gr

grab	grill
grad	grim
graft	grin
gram	grip
grand	grit
grant	grub
grasp	grudge
grass	gruff
Greg	grunt
grid	

gw

Gwen

Lesson 63

pl

plan	pluck		
plank	plug		
plant	plum		
pledge	plump		
plop	plus		
plot	plush		

pr

prance	print
prank	prod
prep	prom
press	prompt
prick	prong
prim	prop
prince	

Lesson 64

sl

slab	slat	sling	sluff
slack	sled	slink	slug
slag	sledge	slip	slum
slam	slept	slop	slump
slant	slick	slosh	slung
slap	slid	slot	slush
slash	slim		

Lesson 65

shr	sm	sn
shrank	smack	snack
shred	small	snag
shrill	smash	snap
shrimp	smell	snick
shrink	smog	sniff
shrub	smudge	snip
shrug	smug	snub
shrunk		snuck
		snug

Lesson 66

sp		spl	spr
Spam	spent	splash	sprang
span	spin	splint	spring
spank	spit	split	sprung
spat	spot	splotch	sprig
speck	spud		sprint
sped	spun		
spell	spunk		
spend			

Lesson 67

st

				str
stab	stank	stilt	stub	strand
stack	stash	sting	stuck	strap
staff	stem	stink	stud	string
stag	step	stint	stuff	strip
stamp	stick	stock	stung	strum
Stan	stiff	stomp	stump	strut
stand	still	stop	stunt	

Lesson 68

sw	**sc**	**sk**	**scr**
swam	scab	skid	scram
swell	scalp	skill	scrap
swept	scam	skim	scratch
swift	scamp	skimp	scrimp
swim	scan	skin	script
swing	scant	skip	scrod
swish	scat	skit	scrub
Swiss	Scott	skunk	scrunch
switch	scuff		
swan			
swamp			

77

Lesson 69

tr

track	trek	trip	trump
tram	trench	trod	trunk
trance	trend	trot	trust
trap	trick	truck	
trash	trim	trudge	

thr

thrall	throb
thrash	throng
thresh	thrush
thrift	thrust
thrill	

tw

twang
twelve
twig
twill
twin
twist
twit
twitch

Lesson 70

truck	jump	bless
skip	then	Dutch
swift	spun	with
quick	slosh	pest
grudge	shrimp	dish
glass	shack	bank
blond	plum	king
fudge	prom	fond
dump	frill	act
task	flag	lift
sash	cliff	left
lisp	crux	kept
clasp	draft	trick
dwell	chest	France
clap	bridge	hitch
slack	edge	next
spring	golf	lunch
witch	elm	flash
smash	scant	twist
snick	scrunch	strand
string	thrush	scuff

Lesson 71

The cat sat still.
Bill had fudge with his lunch.
Patrick drank a glass of milk.
Gwen put cash in the bank.
Pam had a stiff neck.
Kenneth had shrimp for lunch.
The king of France was plump.
Frank is a prince.
The bus stop is on the bridge.
His skin has an itch.
Stan put the trash in the basket.
Fred sat on the grass.
The frog swam in the swamp.
A frog can jump and swim.
A skunk can jump and skip.
The swift skunk stunk.
Madge had a strand of gems.
The clock struck twelve.
The truck got stuck in the mud.

Lesson 72

ă	ā
at	ate
hat	hate
fat	fate
mat	mate
rat	rate
Al	ale
pal	pale
Sal	sale
gal	gale
fad	fade
mad	made
man	mane
Jan	Jane
van	vane
cap	cape
gap	gape

Lesson 73

Long a as a-e

Abe	ace	ade	safe	age
babe	face	fade		cage
	lace	made		page
	pace	wade		rage
	race	blade		sage
	brace	glade		wage
	grace	grade		stage
	place	shade		
	space	spade		
	trace	trade		

Lesson 73

(Continued)

bake	ale	came	cane	ape
cake	bale	dame	Dane	cape
fake	dale	fame	Jane	gape
Jake	hale	game	lane	tape
lake	male	lame	mane	drape
make	pale	name	pane	grape
quake	sale	same	sane	scrape
rake	tale	tame	crane	shape
sake	scale	blame	plane	
take	stale	flame		
wake	whale	frame		
brake		shame		
drake				
flake				
shake				
snake				
stake				
ache				

83

Lesson 73

(Continued)

bare	base	date	cave	daze
care	case	fate	Dave	gaze
dare	chase	gate	gave	haze
fare		hate	pave	maze
hare		Kate	rave	blaze
mare		late	save	craze
rare		mate	wave	glaze
ware		rate	brave	graze
blare		crate	crave	
flare		grate	grave	
glare		plate	shave	
scare		skate	slave	
share		slate	|have|	
snare		state		
spare				
square				
stare				
|are|				

Lesson 74

Jane can bake a cake.
When will Kate wake up and take a bath?
Dave has an ache in his hand.
Bill's rabbit is in a cage.
Dave came, but Kate is late.
Dave ate a date with Kate.
Jane ate the cake.
When will Dave shave his face?
Jack fell in the lake.
Can Dave save Jack?
Yes, Dave is brave.
Dave gave Kate a locket.
This place is safe.
The cat hid in the cave.
His name is Jake.
Kate gave Jane the date of the game.
Abe's face is pale.
Beth ate a grape.

Lesson 75

Long a as ai

aid	ail	aim	Cain	air
laid	bail	claim	gain	fair
maid	fail		lain	hair
paid	Gail		main	pair
raid	hail		pain	chair
braid	jail		rain	Clair
said	mail		vain	stair
	nail		brain	
	pail		chain	bait
	quail		drain	wait
	rail		grain	trait
	tail		plain	
	frail		slain	
	snail		Spain	
	trail		stain	
			strain	
			train	
			again	
			against	

86

Lesson 76

Clair paid ten cents at the gate.
Gail will wait in the rain for the train.
If the train is late, Gail will take a bus.
In Spain the rain falls on the plain.
Cain is waiting at the main gate.
If the train is late, take a plane.
"Fish or cut bait," said Bill.
Gail is washing her hair.
Jane is trimming her nails.
"If it rains, take the train," said Dave.
"It is raining," said Kate.
"Wait for Jane," said Dave. But Kate did not wait in the rain.
The mail is late.
Spring is in the air.

Lesson 77

Long a as ay and ey

bay	may	clay	hey
day	nay	gray	grey
Fay	pay	play	obey
hay	ray	slay	they
Jay	say	spray	
Kay	way	stay	
lay		stray	
		sway	
		tray	

Lesson 78

Can Fay play with Kay?
They say that Fay may play with Kay.
Jay will play a game with Kay.
Fay will stay with Kay all day.
Jay fell in the hay.
They went that way.
They came late that day.
The day was grey.

Lesson 79

Long a as ei and eigh

rein	weigh	reign
vein	sleigh	height
veil	eight	
heir	eighth	
their	weight	
beige	freight	

Bill is eight.

Jack has eight cents.

Kay's hat has a veil.

Dave ate eight cupcakes.

The freight train came.

Can they weigh the freight?

Yes, they can weigh the freight
   on a scale.

They will play with their game.

Dave and Kay are on the eighth
   day of their game.

Lesson 80

face	vale	main	ache	ale
pain	veil	flame	jay	take
way	dare	rain	mail	ail
plate	brave	rein	ate	raid
cage	brain	grade	hate	eight
space	gate	cake	quake	ate
scrape	vein	day	trail	vain
paid	fake	weigh	age	vein
chair	stain	play	wait	freight
their	care	they	made	eighth
tail	brake	say	shade	beige

Lesson 81

vale	veil	vail
rain	rein	reign
vain	vein	vane
main	mane	mein
hail	hale	
ate	eight	
made	maid	
tale	tail	
male	mail	
wait	weight	
way	weigh	

Lesson 82

pay-day	payday
rail-way	railway
air-plane	airplane
space-ship	spaceship
a-way	away
en-gage	engage
wait-ress	waitress
rain-ing	raining
en-slave	enslave
grate-ful	grateful
ex-plain	explain
com-plain	complain
mail-man	mailman
chair-man	chairman
em-brace	embrace
ob-tain	obtain
tail-gate	tailgate
play-mate	playmate

Lesson 83

au and **aw**

Maud	daunt	sauce	awe	hawk
fraud	flaunt	cause	jaw	bawl
haul	gaunt	clause	law	brawl
maul	haunt	pause	paw	crawl
Paul	jaunt	taut	raw	drawl
Saul	taunt	gauze	saw	dawn
fault	haunch		claw	fawn
vault	launch		draw	lawn
	staunch		flaw	pawn
	aunt		thaw	yawn
			slaw	brawn
			straw	drawn

Lesson 84

Paul saw a spot on Saul's jaw.
Paul saw Aunt Maud sitting on
   the lawn.
The cat cut her paw.
Paul drank his milk with a straw.
The dawn came at six o'clock.

Lesson 85

a *as in* ma *and* car

ma	pa	father	haha
mama	papa		java
			lava
			drama

arc	bar	barb	ark	arm	art
ark	car	garb	bark	farm	cart
arm	far		dark	harm	dart
art	jar	bard	hark	charm	mart
	mar	card	lark		part
	tar	hard	mark	barn	tart
	scar	lard	park	darn	chart
	star	yard	Clark	tarn	smart
			shark	yarn	start
	arch	barge	spark		
	march	charge	stark	carp	carve
	starch	large		harp	starve
		Marge	scarf	sharp	
			snarl		

war	warm	warn
ward	warmth	warp
	swarm	wart

quart	dwarf
	wharf

Lesson 86

Mark has a red car.

"Park the car in the yard," said Art.

Pam has a big jar of jam.

Beth has a part in a play.

Mark's farm has a barn.

Father went far away on the plane.

It is dark in the park.

"Start the car," said Ma.

The dog will bark in the dark.

Pa's yard is full of junk.

Mark's arm has an itch.

Beth has a ball of yarn.

"If it rains, put the cart in the barn," said Father.

The shark ate the small fish.

Clark and Mark are smart.

Marge drank a quart of milk.

Paul and Art will play cards.

Mark can take his car apart.

Lesson 87

Long e as ee

bee	deed	leek	deem	deer	fleece
Dee	feed	meek	seem	jeer	Greece
fee	heed	peek	teem	peer	
gee	need	seek		veer	geese
Lee	reed	week	teen	cheer	cheese
see	seed	cheek	keen	sneer	
flee	weed	creek	seen	steer	peeve
free	bleed	Greek	green		sleeve
glee	breed	sleek	queen	beet	
three	creed		screen	feet	breeze
tree	freed		been	meet	freeze
knee	greed	eel		fleet	sneeze
	speed	feel	beep	greet	tweeze
reech		heel	deep	sheet	wheeze
peech	beef	keel	jeep	street	
	reef	peel	keep	sweet	be
		reel	peep	tweet	he
		steel	weep		me
		wheel	creep	teeth	we
		kneel	sheep		she
			sleep		
			steep		
			sweep		

Lesson 88

I see the tree.
Can the tree see me?
She is the queen.
Is she the queen of Greece?
Yes, she is the Greek queen.
We ate beef this week.
Lee came in a jeep.
Will they sweep the street this week?
Yes, they will sweep the street at three.
He is free at three o'clock.
I have seen the queen.
Lee will greet the queen.
Dee and Lee will cheer the queen.
We ate cheese this week.
She ate cheese and beef.
"Meet me next week," she said.
The deer was in a deep sleep.
He was sleeping in the breeze.
Lee was on his knee fixing the jeep.

Lesson 89
Long e as ea

pea	leaf	beam	ear	eat	peace
sea	sheaf	seam	dear	beat	
tea		team	fear	feat	ease
flea	beak	cream	gear	heat	cease
plea	leak	dream	hear	meat	lease
	peak	gleam	near	neat	tease
each	weak	steam	rear	peat	crease
beach	sneak	stream	tear	seat	grease
peach	speak		year	cheat	please
reach	streak	bean	clear	treat	
teach		Jean		wheat	breathe
bleach	deal	lean	leash		
breach	heal	mean			eave
	meal	clean	east		leave
bead	peal		beast		heave
lead	real	heap	feast		weave
read	seal	leap	least		
plead	teal	reap	yeast		
	veal	cheap			
	zeal				
	steal				

Lesson 89

(Continued)

sweat	realm	bear	dead	steak
threat	dealt	pear	head	break
sweater		tear	lead	great
		wear	read	
		swear	bread	
			breath	
			deaf	
			meant	

Lesson 90

Jean had a dream. She put cream in her tea.
Jean ate a meal of veal, peas, bread, and tea.
Then she ate a peach. The peach was sweet.
Bill is at sea. The sea is in the east.
The beach is neat and clean.
Jean sat in her seat. The seat is near
   the rear.
Bill is on the team this year.
The dog has fleas. The cat is neat and clean.
When will we reach the beach?
Steak will be great. Let's break for steak.
Jean will read "The Seal Had Zeal."

Lesson 91

Long e as e-e

gene	here	eve	Pete
scene	mere	Steve	theme
there	were	Swede	these
where			eye

Where is Steve?
Steve is here.
Where were Pete and Steve?
Pete and Steve were here.
Here is where they were.
Where were they?
They were here and there.
"Sit here, not there," said Steve.
Steve and Gene were there at the beach.
The sun was in Steve's eyes.
Steve had a tear in his eye.
Eve has green eyes.

Lesson 92

Long e as ie

brief	field	pier	fiend
chief	yield	tier	niece
grief	wield	fierce	piece
thief	shield	pierce	siege
			sieze
Jackie	Minnie	Bonnie	friend
Lassie	Vinnie	Connie	receive
Debbie		Ronnie	

Debbie and Ronnie sat on the pier.

Jackie is Connie's friend.

Vinnie and Ronnie are friends.

Lassie ran in the field.

The thief ran away. Vinnie will sieze the thief.

The heat from the sun is fierce.

Bonnie shields her eyes from the sun.

Connie has a niece. Her name is Minnie.

Lesson 93

Long e as y

Abby	daddy	taffy	baggy	Billy
Tabby	caddy	daffy	saggy	Sally
Libby	paddy	jiffy	Maggy	silly
lobby	Teddy	puffy	foggy	Molly
Debby	muddy	stuffy	Peggy	Polly
baby	study		muggy	chilly
		Harry		daily
mammy	Danny	carry	messy	
mommy	Denny	Barry	sissy	Betty
mummy	Lanny	Perry	fussy	batty
tummy	Benny	Terry	easy	catty
Tommy	Jenny	merry		fatty
Timmy	Lenny	hurry	busy	nutty
Jimmy	Kenny	sorry		putty
Sammy	penny	Gary	hazy	city
	bunny	marry	lazy	pity
happy	funny	berry	crazy	
pappy	sunny	cherry	dizzy	pretty
peppy		very	fuzzy	
poppy	money	furry		candy
puppy	any	worry	key	handy
	many			sandy

Lesson 94

Billy was silly.
Taffy was daffy.
Mommy was happy.
Daddy was very merry.
Danny ate candy.
Kenny felt dizzy.
The lobby was stuffy.
The day is hot and muggy.
The bunny is funny.
Larry is dizzy.
Debbie is very pretty.
Betty is busy.
Jerry is in a hurry.
The day was chilly and foggy.
Perry is very sorry.
Gary hasn't any money.
The city is hilly.
The day was sunny.
Daddy was busy.
The baby was fussy.
Can Perry carry Barry?

Lesson 95

baby	babies	lobby	lobbies
berry	berries	cherry	cherries
city	cities	bunny	bunnies
puppy	puppies	candy	candies
penny	pennies	hurry	hurries
marry	marries	study	studies

Lesson 96

tea	easy	queen	steer	eel
week	jeep	reach	greasy	ease
fear	tree	sweet	hear	clear
beet	he	sea	meat	city
see	key	field	steal	beach
dear	please	she	feet	read
year	gear	study	meet	tease
here	near	Pete	chief	feel
niece	thief	treat	cheer	peace
greet	mean	need	bean	seat
these	we	eve	weep	breeze
sleep	leaf	leap	creep	street

Lesson 97

The street is neat and clean.
Lee's feet need rest.
Peggy feels very sleepy.
"Meet me at the beach," Betty said.
Where is the beach?
The beach is near the city.
"Please teach me to read," Pete said
   to his teacher.
There is a breeze near the sea.
We can sleep on the beach and feel
   the sea breeze.
There are trees near the sea.
"There are three peach trees in the
   field near Berry Street," said Gene.
Steve can reach a peach with ease.
The berries are sweet.
"For Pete's sake, hurry up," said Jean.
We will be back at the beach next week.
"Did Lee hear me?" asked Billy.
"Where are the keys?" asked Penny.
Steve will pick the cherries from the tree.
It is easy to read this page.

Lesson 98

Long i as I, y, ie and uy

I am	by	shy	die	buy
I can	my	sky	lie	guy
I take	cry	sly	pie	
I had	dry	spry	tie	
I have	fly	spy		
I ran	fry	sty		
	pry	try		
		why		

I will dry my wet tie.

"I can not tell a lie," said Terry.

"I will try to do better," said John.

Why did the big guy cry?

Jack's dad will fly in the plane to Spain.

She had cherry pie for lunch.

"Can you tie the bow on my dress?" Connie asked.

"I will fry an egg for Timmy," said Mom.

Lesson 99

Long i as i-e

ice	bide	file	dine	fire	dive
dice	hide	mile	fine	hire	five
lice	ride	Nile	line	mire	hive
mice	side	pile	mine	tire	jive
nice	tide	tile	nine	wire	live
rice	wide	smile	pine	spire	chive
vice	bride	while	vine		drive
price	glide	isle	wine	bite	strive
slice	slide	aisle	shine	kite	give
spice	stride		spine	mite	live
twice		dime	swine	quite	
	life	lime	thine	site	rise
bribe	wife	mime	twine	spite	wise
tribe	strife	time	shrine	sprite	
	knife	chime	whine	trite	size
		crime		white	prize
		grime	pipe		
		slime	ripe		
			wipe		
			gripe		
			swipe		
			stripe		

Lesson 99

(Continued)

I like red berry ice cream.
I can ride my bike to the pike.
I will fly my kite at the beach.
We ate a slice of pie.
I will strive to do my best.
We will strive to run a mile each day.
Danny will fix the tire on his bike.
Jenny has a pretty smile.
"Let's play hide and seek," said Jake.
What time is it? It is five o'clock.
Mike likes to ride his bike. Tim likes to drive his car.
They won a nice prize at the fair.
Jean is Jack's wife.
Her doll can cry like a baby.
Mom and Jan like plain rice, but Dad likes spice on his rice.
"I feel fine," Betty said.

Lesson 100

Long i as igh

high	fight	tight
sigh	light	bright
thigh	might	flight
	night	fright
	right	slight
	sight	

The light was bright.
The price is right.
The night was chilly.
Is the price high?
Yes, the price is very high.
The fire is bright.
Land is in sight.
The bright lights of the city are a sight at night.
Mike was in a prize fight.
Mike fights with all his might.
The sky is bright tonight.

Lesson 101

ough *and* **augh**

ought	fought	caught
bought	sought	taught
brought	thought	daughter
	though	slaughter

I bought candy and gum.
Paul caught the ball.
He thought the ball was fast.
Dad taught a tennis lesson.

Lesson 102

f *as* **gh**

rough	laugh
tough	laughing
cough	laughter
coughing	

Dad has a cough.
Mom gave him a cough drop.
The steak was tough.
Mike made Billy laugh.
The sea was rough.

Lesson 103

Long o as o-e

robe	hole	bone	cope	hose	cove
lobe	mole	cone	hope	pose	dove
globe	pole	lone	mope	rose	rove
probe	role	tone	rope	chose	wove
	sole	zone	grope	close	drove
code	stole	phone	scope	prose	grove
mode	whole	stone	slope	those	stove
rode	soul	throne			move
		one	bore	dose	prove
joke	dome	once	core	close	
poke	home	none	more		dove
woke	Rome	done	tore	lose	love
yoke	come		sore	whose	glove
broke	some	gone	wore		shove
choke			chore	note	
smoke			score	rote	owe
spoke			shore	tote	
stroke			snore	vote	doze
			store	quote	froze

Lesson 104

My nose is sore.

My home is in Rome.

I spoke on the phone.

I had an ice cream cone.

I love a joke.

Tell me a funny joke.

She will move the stone one more time.

The stove is hot.

The dog ate the bone.

Perry wore a bathrobe.

Jean woke up. Then she woke me up.

A rose is a rose. A rose smells nice.

Dad drove to the store.

He bought some hotdogs and a Coke.

"Come home when you are done," she said.

Mom ate something for lunch.

Betty loves to talk on the phone.

"Tell me more," she said in a soft tone.

I sent Kathy a note. The note was in code.

"Please don't poke and shove," Tom said.

We chose to go to the seashore.

Lesson 105

Long o as oa

load	oak	Joan	oat	boast
road	soak	loan	boat	coast
toad	cloak		coat	roast
broad		oar	goat	toast
	coal	roar	bloat	
coach	goal	soar	float	coax
poach		board		hoax
	foam	source	soap	
loaf	roam	court		
		course		

The car is on the road.

He bought a loaf of bread.

Joan ate a roast beef sandwich.

The soap can float.

Dad bought coal for the stove.

Jan and Joan had oatmeal.

Mom has tea and toast each day.

Dad bought a big boat.

The boat floats on the lake.

Joan wore her red coat.

Lesson 106

Long o as ow

bow	know	show	bowl	grown
low	blow	slow		known
mow	crow	snow	own	shown
row	flow	stow	blown	thrown
sow	glow	throw	flown	growth
tow	grow	dough		
owe		though		

Joan wants to grow up.
The snow fell last night.
I know what I want.
I want to own a car.
Bill wants his own boat.
Bob wants to row his boat.
Go slow in the snow.
"I know the way home," said Joan.
Jack will mow the lawn after lunch.
Mom gave the cat a bowl of milk.
Dad and Mike like to go bowling on Sundays.
Mike has grown up.
We saw a TV show.
Bonnie has shown a lot of growth.
The ball was thrown to Jim.

Lesson 107

Long o *as in* old

old	hold	host	oh	only
bold	mold	most	go	Joe
cold	sold	post	no	doe
fold	told	cost	so	
gold	scold	lost	quo	
			yo-yo	

The old home was cold.
"Hold my hand," she said.
"Go home," I told him.
He was lost.
He sold his home.
I know what he told her.
In winter it is cold most of the time.
Bob sold his gold ring.
I told him so.
Dad sold his boat.
It had cost him a lot of money.
"It was only money," he said.
He is the only one I know with a boat.
Most of the time he stays home.
"Go slow. There is ice on the road," said Dad.

Lesson 108

to		do		young
too		who		
two		you		
		youth		

Do you know who went to the phone?
Did you do what you were told?
The two of you must know what to do.
Who do you think you are?
Do you know who you are?
I want to go too.
You are young.
You are too young to go alone.
The box is two feet high.
It is too big.
Give it back to him.
What shall I do?
Go to the man who sold it to you.

Lesson 109

oo *as in* **good food**

coo	spook	boom	boon	coop	boot
boo		doom	moon	loop	coot
moo	cool	room	noon	hoop	hoot
too	fool	zoom	soon	droop	loot
woo	pool	bloom	spoon	scoop	root
zoo	tool	broom		snoop	toot
	drool	gloom	groove	stoop	shoot
food	school	groom	ooze	troop	
mood	stool		snooze		roost
		loose		booth	
goof	stooge	moose		tooth	soup
roof		noose		smooth	group
proof		choose			

good	hoof	book	nook	cook
hood	wool	hook	brook	cookie
wood	foot	look	crook	cookies
stood	soot	took	shook	

boor	door	flood
poor	floor	blood
moor		

116

Lesson 110

Joan and Jane went to the zoo.
The zoo was too far from home.
Jane took a book with her.
Joan wore a wool coat.
Soon they will go to school.
The pool was cool, but the food was good.
Betty can cook good food.
Jim stood at the door and took a look.
Look at Betty's room. It's so neat.
"Open the door," said Pam. "I have cookies and milk."
The door is made of wood.
The dentist said my tooth was loose.
Barry sat on the floor. He took a snooze.
It's noon. Time for lunch.
Betty has too much to do this afternoon.
The broom is in Mike's bedroom.
Go to his room and get it.
Soon it will be noon.
Choose a good book to read.

Lesson 111

ould sounding as **ood** in **wood**

could	→	could not	→	couldn't
would	→	would not	→	wouldn't
should	→	should not	→	shouldn't

I would go if I could.
If he could go, he would.
Couldn't I go?
He could go, but not the two of you.
I would like to go, but I know I shouldn't.
Should I go? No, you should stay.
Shawn has a bad cold.
Should he go to school?
He shouldn't go to school if he has a cold.
I wouldn't go if I had a bad cold.
If I were sick I would stay in bed.
Would you?
Yes, I would.

Lesson 112

ow and ou as in cow and ouch

bow	brow	owl	down	browse	bower
cow	chow	cowl	gown		cower
how	plow	fowl	town	towel	power
now		howl	brown	trowel	tower
pow	crowd	jowl	clown	vowel	flower
sow		growl	crown		shower
vow		prowl	drown		
wow			frown		

ouch	loud	bough	our	house	out
couch	cloud	plough	hour	louse	bout
pouch	proud	drought	sour	mouse	pout
vouch			flour	blouse	scout
crouch	bound	rough	four	spouse	shout
slouch	found	tough	pour		snout
touch	hound	enough	tour	mouth	spout
	mound		your	south	stout
noun	pound	doubt	fourth	youth	trout
ounce	round		mourn		
ounce	sound				count
ounce	wound				fount
	ground				
	wound				

119

Lesson 113

How did the cow get out of the house?
A mouse let her out.
"I found the cow near the house," Brother said.
They heard a loud sound.
The house fell down.
"Ouch," said the clown.
The clown ran out of the house.
They went downtown.
It took an hour to find the cow.
The cow was in a crowd, and then she went around the tower.
How now brown cow? Will you come home?
"Not now," said the cow. "Bow wow," said the dog.
A man came to the house. "Your cow is in town," he said.
The clown chased the mouse round and round.

Lesson 114

oy as in **boy**, **oi** as in **oil**

boy	oil	coin	noise	hoist
coy	boil	join	poise	foist
joy	coil	loin		moist
Roy	foil	void	choice	
soy	soil	joint	voice	
toy	toil	point		
Joyce	broil			
Royce	spoil			

poi-son	poison	joy-ful	joyful
oil-y	oily	boy-ish	boyish
an-noy	annoy	broil-ing	broiling

Roy gave the toy to Joyce.
The cat likes to annoy Joyce.
Roy wants to join a club.
He has a choice of two clubs.
Joyce has a jar of coins.
Roy has a ballpoint pen.
The water is about to boil.
The soil is moist.
Joyce made a good point.
Uncle Royce has a boyish smile.

Lesson 115

Long u as u-e

cube	dude	duke	fume	cure	cute
lube	Jude	juke	spume	pure	jute
Rube	rude	Luke	plume	lure	lute
tube	crude	fluke		sure	mute
	prude		dune		brute
Bruce		mule	June	use	flute
truce	dupe	rule	tune	fuse	
spruce	huge	yule	prune	muse	

June can play a tune on the flute.
Luke sat on the sand dune.
June ate a prune.
Luke rode on a mule.
June is cute.
The cloud was huge.
Luke put a dime in the jukebox.
Is there a cure for a cold?
We are not sure.
If there is a cure, let's use it.
Bruce has a tube of toothpaste.
Dad put a fuse in the fuse box.
It's never nice to be rude.

Lesson 116

Long u as ue and ui

cue	blue	flu	juice
due	clue		bruise
hue	flue	queue	cruise
Sue	glue		
cruel	true		suit
duel			fruit
fuel			

Sue had prune juice at breakfast.

Is it true that Sue has the flu?

Yes, it's true.

Take a cue from Sue. When you have a cold, eat lots of fruit and drink lots of juice.

Sue's dress is blue.

Bruce has a tube of glue.

He will use the glue to fix a toy.

Lesson 117

Long u as ew and eu

dew	blew	grew	slew	feud
few	brew	stew	threw	deuce
Lew	chew	view		
mew	clew	knew	through	
new	crew	screw		
news	drew			
pew	flew			
sew				

June has a new dress.
What's new?
The news is good.
Good news is always nice.
Tell me the good news.
Lew is having beef stew.
I knew the news was good.
Sue likes to chew gum.
She grew an inch.
Luke threw a stone.
He threw it far.
Lew drew a cat on his sketchpad.
Sue will sew her blue coat.

Lesson 118

er, ir, or, ur and ear

her	perch	fir	dirt	fur	lurch
verb	clerk	sir	flirt	curb	urge
herd	merge	bird	shirt	surf	purge
perk	verge	gird	skirt	turf	splurge
germ	terse	girl	squirt	lurk	surge
term	verse	third	thirst	Turk	curse
fern	nerve	shirk	birth	hurl	nurse
Vern	serve	smirk	mirth	urn	purse
Bert	verve	chirp		burn	curve
pert				turn	burnt
				hurt	burst

earn	word	birth-day	birthday
learn	work	thirst-y	thirsty
yearn	worm	tur-nip	turnip
heard	worst	tur-key	turkey
pearl	worth	ex-pert	expert
search		home-work	homework
earth			

Lesson 118

(Continued)

Sue wants to be a nurse.
Bert likes to throw curve balls.
He is in his third year of baseball.
Today is Vern's birthday.
Willy likes to learn new words.
He is an expert at learning verses.
Kelly is sitting on the curb.
Bonnie has curls in her hair.
She is holding a purse in her lap.
Mom will grow turnips in her garden.
We will have turkey for dinner.
"Did you do your homework?" Dad asked.
Vinnie will work with his list of words.
The clerk wore a new shirt.
The girl lost her purse.
Bert held the bird and heard it sing.
The bird was hurt and thirsty.
Bert will urge Vern to get water for the bird.

Lesson 119

words ending in **le**

able	babble	dazzle	tattle	ample
cable	bubble	fizzle	turtle	sample
fable	pebble	drizzle	single	simple
table	apple	wiggle	jingle	dimple
stable	grapple	jiggle	jungle	pimple
eagle	paddle	battle	bangle	temple
beagle	faddle	bottle	dangle	fumble
idle	saddle	cattle	bungle	bumble
rifle	fiddle	little	juggle	humble
trifle	riddle	settle	struggle	tumble
stifle	raffle	kettle	strangle	handle
title	ruffle	brittle	skittle	candle

silent **t**: hustle, bustle, rustle

He ate a little apple. He threw a pebble.
She had a little dimple. He sat at the table.
He had a pimple on his dimple.
She was nimble with a thimble.
The bottle was brittle.
The candle was on the table.
Can a beagle chase an eagle?
Can a turtle play a fiddle?
Are you able to handle a paddle?
The drizzle was a fizzle.
There was a battle in the jungle.

Lesson 120

f as **ph**

Phil	phone	phantom	photograph
Philip	phony	pharmacy	telegraph
	photo	pharmacist	telephone
Ralph	phonics	Philadelphia	graphic
graph	Phoenix	philosopher	emphasis
	phase	philosophy	emphatic
	phrase		

Lesson 121

sh as **ti**   **sh** as **ssi**, **ci**, and **ce**

nation	patient	fission	racial
station	patience	mission	facial
ration	action	admission	special
lotion	fraction	session	crucial
motion	traction		musician
notion			ocean

sh as **ci**, **sci**, and **xi**   **sh** as **su** and **ssu**

atrocious	obnoxious	sure	issue
ferocious		insure	tissue
conscious		assure	
conscience		fissure	

Lesson 121

(Continued)

zh *as* **si** *and* **su**		**ch** *as* **tu** *and* **ti**	
fusion	measure	capture	question
confusion	pleasure	fracture	digestion
illusion	treasure	gesture	indigestion
intrusion	leisure	picture	suggestion

The ocean can be ferocious.
Ralph is a musician and won a special prize at the fair.
Jeff went to the train station to pick up Kate.
Did you see Gail's picture on the table?
Betty had a crucial question for the teacher.
"Thank you for being so patient," said Dad.
Mom bought a box of facial tissues.
She phoned the pharmacy for special lotion.
Didn't you think that motion picture was obnoxious?
It sure was a pleasure to see Grandma and Grandpa this weekend.
Grandma brought an album of photographs from Phoenix, which we will treasure.
Dad will measure the wood to a fraction of an inch.
The doctor's suggestion cleared Philip's confusion about his indigestion.

Lesson 122

n as kn

knee	knit	knack	know
kneel	knitting	knock	known
kneeling	knitted	knob	knowing
knelt	knife	knot	knowledge
	knight	knuckle	knew
		knickers	

Lesson 123

m as mb

lamb	bomb	comb
jamb	bombed	combed
dumb	bombing	combing
numb	climb	plumber
crumb	climbed	plumbing
thumb	climbing	tomb

t as bt: debt, doubt

Lesson 124

silent h

hour	ghost	rhyme
honor	ghastly	rhymed
honest	ghetto	rhyming
heir	ghoul	

Lesson 125

r as wr

write	wrap	wrench	wrangle
writer	wrack	wretch	wrinkle
writing	wrath	wretched	wring
written	wreck	wriggle	wrong
wrote	wreath	wriggled	wrung
wrist	wrought	wriggling	wry

Lesson 126

s as st   f as ft

castle	listen	wrestle	often
nestle	listener	wrestled	soften
hasten	listening	wrestler	softener
moisten	whistle	wrestling	softening
fasten	whistler		

Lesson 127

k as ch   s as ps

character	chorus	scheme	psychic
choir	choral	schedule	psyche
Christmas	chord	school	
	chlorine	scholar	
chemist	chronic	scholastic	
chemistry	chronicle		

Lesson 128

y as short i

cyst	gymnast	gymnasium
gym	mystic	mystery
hymn	system	syllable
Lynn	symbol	sympathy
myth	symptom	synonym
	rhythm	hysteric
	syrup	hypnosis
	lyric	cylinder
	syntax	typical
	Phyllis	tyranny
	Sheryl	synthetic
	cryptic	mystical
	physic	physical
	physics	physician

ORDER OF LESSONS

Lessons

1. Short **a**; consonants **m, n, s, t, x**
2. Initial consonants **S, m, h, s, t**
3. Review sentences
4. Consonants **d, D, w**
5. Alphabetic word building
6. Short **a** sentences; punctuation
7. Word building with short **a**; consonant **l**
8. Consonants **l, b, c, g, f, j, l, n**
9. Consonants **p, r, t, v, w, y, z**; final consonant **k**
10. Review of short **a** words
11. Consonant digraph **ck; qu**
12. **a** as a word
13. Sentences
14. Nonsense syllables with **short a**
15. Short vowels **a, e, i, o, u**
16. Short **e** words
17. Short **e** sentences
18. Nonsense syllables with **short e**
19. Short **i** words; **f** as **ph**
20. Short **i** sentences
21. Consonant digraph **th**
22. Sentences
23. Short **o** words
24. Short **o** sentences
25. Plural **s, es**, and **'s**
26. Sentences
27. Short **u** words
28. Short **u** sentences
28a. Consonants **b** and **d**
29. Consonant digraph **sh**
30. Consonant digraph **ch**
31. Consonant digraph **wh**
32. Review of **sh, ch, wh** words
33. Sentences
34. Verbs **to be** and **to have**
35. Sentences with verbs **to be** and **to have**
36. Contractions
37. Sentences with contractions
38. Two-syllable, short vowel words
39. Sentences with two-syllable, short-vowel words
40. **a** as in **all**; sentences
41. Consonant blend **ng; ing** words

42. Sentences with **ing** words
43. Final consonant blends **nd, nt**
44. Sentences
45. Final syllable **er; er** words and sentences
46. Final consonant blends **nk, nc, nch**
47. Sentences
48. Final consonant blends **ct, ft, pt, xt**; sentences
49. Final consonant blends **sk, sp, st**; sentences
50. Final consonant blends **lb, ld, lf, lk**
51. Final consonant blends **lm, lp, lt**
52. Final consonant blend **mp**
53. Final consonant blend **tch**; sentences
54. Final consonant blends **dge, nge**
55. Final consonant blends **nce, nse**
56. Review of words with final consonant blends
57. Two-syllable words with consonant blends
58. Initial consonant blends **bl, br**
59. Initial consonant blends **cl, cr**
60. Initial consonant blends **dr, dw**
61. Initial consonant blends **fl, fr**
62. Initial consonant blends **gl, gr, gw**
63. Initial consonant blends **pl, pr**
64. Initial consonant blend **sl**
65. Initial consonant blends **shr, sm, sn**
66. Initial consonant blends **sp, spl, spr**
67. Initial consonant blends **st, str**
68. Initial consonant blends **sw, sc, sk, scr**
69. Initial consonant blends **tr, thr, tw**
70. Words with consonant blends
71. Sentences
72. Long **a**
73. Long **a** as **a-e**
74. Sentences
75. Long **a** as **ai**
76. Sentences
77. Long **a** as **ay** and **ey**
78. Sentences
79. Long **a** as **ei** and **eigh**; sentences
80. Review of words with long **a** spellings
81. Long **a** homonyms
82. Two-syllable words with long **a** syllables
83. Vowel spellings **au** and **aw**
84. Sentences with **au** and **aw** words
85. **a** as in **ma** and **car**

86. Sentences
87. Long **e** as **ee**
88. Sentences
89. Long **e** as **ea**
90. Sentences
91. Long **e** as **e-e**; sentences
92. Long **e** as **ie**; sentences
93. Long **e** as **y**
94. Sentences
95. **ies** in verbs and plural nouns
96. Review of long **e** words
97. Sentences
98. Long **i** as **I**, **y**, **ie**, **uy**; sentences
99. Long **i** as **i-e**; sentences
100. Long **i** as **igh**; sentences
101. Spelling forms **ough** and **augh**
102. **f** as **gh**
103. Long **o** as **o-e**
104. Sentences
105. Long **o** as **oa**; sentences
106. Long **o** as **ow**; sentences
107. Long **o** as in **old**; sentences
108. Common irregular words; sentences
109. **oo** as in **good food**
110. Sentences
111. **ould** sounding as **ood** in **wood**; sentences
112. **ow** and **ou** as in **cow** and **ouch**
113. Sentences
114. **oy** as in **boy**; **oi** as in **oil**; sentences
115. Long **u** as **u-e**; sentences
116. Long **u** as **ue** and **ui**; sentences
117. Long **u** as **ew** and **eu**; sentences
118. **er**, **ir**, **or**, **ur**, **ear**; sentences
119. Words ending in **le**; silent **t**; sentences
120. **f** as **ph**
121. **sh** as **ti**, **ssi**, **ci**, **ce**, **sci**, **xi**, **su**, **ssu**; **zh** as **si**, **su**; **ch** as **tu**, **ti**; sentences
122. **n** as **kn**
123. **m** as **mb**; **t** as **bt**
124. Silent **h**
125. **r** as **wr**
126. **s** as **st**; **f** as **ft**
127. **k** as **ch**; **s** as **ps**
128. **y** as short **i**

135

ENGLISH ALPHABETIC SYSTEM
COMMON SPELLING FORMS

Sound

Vowels

short **a**	**a** as in **cat**
short **e**	**e** as in **met**; **ea** as in **bread**
short **i**	**i** as in **sit**; **y** as in **myth**, **gym**
short **o**	**o** as in **top**
short **u**	**u** as in **cup**; **ou** as in **precious**
long **a**	**a-e** as in **ate**; **ai** as in **wait**; **ay** as in **way**; **ei** as in **veil**; **eigh** as in **eight**; **a** as in **apron**; **ey** as in **they**
long **e**	**ee** as in **tree**; **ea** as in **eat**; **ie** as in **field**; **e** as in **me**; **e-e** as in **eve**; **y** as in **happy**, **city**; **ei** as in **receive**
long **i**	**i-e** as in **time**; **igh** as in **high**; **y** as in **try**; **ie** as in **lie**; **i** as in **item**
long **o**	**o** as in **go**; **o-e** as in **home**; **oa** as in **boat**; **ow** as in **snow**; **oe** as in **toe**
long **u**	**u-e** as in **use**; **ew** as in **new**; **ue** as in **true**; **iew** as in **view**
oo	**oo** as in **food**
oo	**oo** as in **good**; **oul** as in **could**, **should**
ou/ow	**ou** as in **out**; **ow** as in **cow**
oi/oy	**oi** as in **oil**; **oy** as in **boy**
a (ah)	**a** as in **car**, **father**
a	**a** as in **care**, **there**, **heir**, **fair**
a/au/aw	**a** as in **all**; **aw** as in **law**; **au** as in **cause**; **ough** as in **ought**; **augh** as in **taught**; **o** as in **loss**
er	**er** as in **germ**; **ir** as in **girl**; **ur** as in **fur**; **ear** as in **earn**; **or** as in **work**
o	**o** as in **born**, **core**

Consonants

b	b as in **bat**, **cab**
d	d as in **did**
f	f as in **fan**; ph as in **phone**; gh as in **rough**, **laugh**
g	g as in **get**; gh as in **ghetto**
h	h as in **house**; wh as in **who**
j	j as in **jam**, g as in **gem**, **angel**, **ginger**; dge as in **fudge**
k	k/ck as in **kick**; c as in **cat**; ch as in **chorus**; qu as kw (**quit** = **kwit**); x as ks (**rex** = **wrecks**)
l	l as in **lull**
m	m as in **mom**
n	n as in **nut**; kn as in **knee** ng as in **sing**; nk as in **sink**
p	p as in **pep**
r	r as in **ran**, **car**; wr as in **wrap**, **write**
s	s as in **sell**; c as in **cell**; ps as in **psychic**
t	t as in **ten**, **net**
v	v as in **van**, **have**; f as in **of**
w	w as in **well**
y	y as in **yes**
z	z as in **zoo**; s as in **has**
th	th as in **the**, **with**, **father** th as in **thin**, **think**, **truth**
ch	ch as in **chin**, **rich**; tch as in **catch**; tu as in **capture**, **picture**; ti as in **question**
sh	sh as in **she**, **wish**; ti as in **nation**, **patient**; su as in **sure**; ci as in **special**, **precious**; ce as in **ocean**; ssi as in **mission**; sci as in **conscious**; xi as in **noxious**; ssu as in **issue**
wh	wh as in **where**, **when**
zh	su as in **pleasure**; si as in **fusion**

Cursive Alphabet

Introducing Cursive

One of the most important tools of literacy that an individual must acquire is good cursive handwriting. Cursive is a flowing form of handwriting in which all the letters of a word are joined. Manuscript, or print-script, which most children are taught in the first grade, is really a form of hand printing or lettering.

Most schools require children to learn cursive by the third grade. Unfortunately, many children fail to make a good transition from manuscript to cursive mainly because the third-grade curriculum does not provide enough time for or supervision over handwriting development. The result is a poor, often illegible handwriting.

But the simple truth is that most children can be taught cursive in the first grade, thereby eliminating the need for a difficult and chancy transition period in the third grade.

The virtue of teaching cursive in the first grade is that the teacher can spend more time supervising its correct acquisition. Also, students will begin developing an active tool of literacy, which they will be using for the rest of their lives.

The most important task for the parent or tutor in teaching cursive is to make sure that the student learns to hold the writing instrument correctly and form the letters correctly; that is, knowing where the letter starts and where it ends.

Cursive was developed to permit writers to obtain a fast, fluent, legible script with minimum expenditure of energy. It takes time to develop a good cursive handwriting, and that is why it is wise to begin cursive instruction in the first grade.

Most children, as they learn the letter forms, begin writing cursive in a large awkward scrawl. This is quite natural because the child is being required to perform a manual physical task, which requires considerable dexterity and precision. But in a few weeks or months, that scrawl will evolve into a neat, legible script.

There are some youngsters – and adults – who experience great difficulty in learning to write. This is usually a physical problem that has nothing to do with intelligence. This condition is called dysgraphia and can only be overcome with a great deal of practice and perseverance. Dysgraphics usually find it equally hard to learn manuscript as well as cursive. Therefore, it makes sense to concentrate on cursive, since ultimately it is the more useful and required tool of literacy.

It is very important to teach the learner to form the letters correctly the first time, for there is nothing more difficult than trying to break bad habits once they are acquired. Such future agony can be avoided by having the child do it right the first time.

For additional information about teaching cursive see Don Potter at DonPotter.net.

Aa Bb Cc Dd Ee
Ff Gg Hh Ii Jj
Kk Ll Mm Nn
Oo Pp Qq Rr Ss
Tt Uu Vv Ww
Xx Yy Zz

About the Author

Samuel L. Blumenfeld is one of the world's leading authorities on the teaching of reading. He has spent over forty years writing on American education and has lectured in all fifty states and in Canada, England, Australia, and New Zealand. He is the author of *The New Illiterates, How to Tutor, Homeschooling: A Parent's Guide to Teaching Children, The Victims of Dick and Jane,* and six other books on education. He writes a column for *Practical Homeschooling* and has written hundreds of articles for WorldNetDaily and The New American online. Mr. Blumenfeld has been a guest on hundreds of radio and television talk shows.

After graduating from the City College of New York in 1950, Mr. Blumenfeld studied at the Sorbonne in Paris. On his return to the U.S., he entered the book publishing industry where he worked at Rinehart and Company, World Publishing Company, The Viking Press, and Grosset & Dunlap, where he served as editor of the Universal Library quality paperback series. He also served as chairman of the Massachusetts branch of the Reading Reform Foundation for twenty years. Mr. Blumenfeld has taught in public and private schools and has tutored extensively.

In 1983, Mr. Blumenfeld created his phonetic reading system, *Alpha-Phonics: A Primer for Beginning Readers*, which for the last 30 years has achieved great popularity among homeschoolers in the United States and abroad. His direct, simple, logical method has taught thousands of children and adults to read.

Phonics for Success was created to make the best and most effective reading program available at the lowest cost to those parents in the urban underclass who need a simple but superior means of helping their children achieve high literacy. It is hoped that *Phonics for Success* will help millions of children acquire the highest literacy skills so that they can escape from poverty by taking part in our dynamic information-based economy in productive, creative, and well-paying careers.

Blumenfeld's

Phonics for Success

The Road to High Literacy

Samuel L. Blumenfeld

We now live and work in a global information-based economy where knowledge is king. *Phonics for Success* gives every child super easy access to that knowledge.

Instruction Manual

TABLE OF CONTENTS

Introduction..........1
Our Alphabetic System..........4
Teaching the Alphabet..........6
Teaching the Letter Sounds..........8
Isolating the Letter Sounds..........10
Suggestions on Writing Instruction..........10
Lesson Instructions: 1-128..........12-37
What Comes After Phonics for Success?..........37

INTRODUCTION

This course of instruction will enable any parent, teacher, or tutor to teach reading to anyone who needs to learn it: beginning readers of all ages or poor readers in need of retraining. The method is based on a thorough analysis of the English writing system, how it works, and how best it can be taught.

Written English is a purely alphabetic system, regardless of what we may think of its many eccentricities and irregularities. An alphabet, by definition, is a set of graphic symbols that stands for the irreducible speech sounds of a particular language. Therefore, all of our written words stand for spoken sounds, no matter how irregular the spellings may be. Incidentally, an irreducible speech sound is an isolated vowel or consonant sound.

We must not forget that the invention of the alphabet is based on one of man's greatest discoveries: that all of spoken language is composed of a relatively small number of different, irreducible speech sounds. (In English, only 44!)

This is one of the great discoveries that has enabled man to do much more with much less. Instead of wrestling with a writing system using thousands and thousands of symbols representing thousands of individual ideas and words, as in Chinese characters or Egyptian hieroglyphics, man could create a writing system using less than fifty symbols to handle an entire language.

It is vitally important to understand the difference between an alphabetic writing system and an ideographic one. An ideographic system uses graphic symbols to represent ideas, feelings, actions, things, etc. It is basically independent of any particular spoken language although its symbols may represent specific words of a language. For example, the "no-smoking" icon (the cigarette in a circle with a slash through it) is an ideograph representing an idea. It can be interpreted by the viewer as "no smoking," "smoking not permitted," "smoking forbidden," or in French as *"defense de fumer,"* in Spanish as *"no fumar,"* or in German as *"nicht rauchen."* In an ideographic system, language is used to interpret the symbols. Precision and accuracy are therefore hard to achieve with an ideographic system.

An alphabetic system, on the other hand, is a sound-symbol system used merely to represent on paper a particular spoken language. The spoken words stand for the ideas, concepts, feelings, etc., while the written words are mere graphic representations of the spoken words. Therefore, in an alphabetic system, the relationship between written and spoken language is one of <u>precision</u> and <u>exactness</u>. The spoken word may be subject to interpretation, but the written word is an exact representation of a specific spoken counterpart. Thus, alphabetic writing is an important tool of thought, for the thought process uses the spoken language for its development.

The invention of the alphabet, which took place about 2000 B.C., not only made hieroglyphics and every other ideographic system obsolete, it permitted a tremendous expansion of vocabulary because now there was a writing system that could easily accommodate it. The greatest works of the ancient world have come down to us through alphabetic writing: the *Iliad*, the *Odyssey*, the Greek dramas, the Bible. Without the alphabet, man's intellectual and spiritual development would have been seriously retarded. So we must regard the alphabet with great awe and respect. It is civilization's prize possession.

It stands to reason that a thorough knowledge and understanding of the English alphabetic system will enable a student not only to read well, but also to spell well. We often forget that our writing system is a two-way process: to be used both for reading **and** writing, decoding and encoding; and to become truly literate, a student must become proficient in both.

Knowledge alone, however, does not lead to reading fluency. To gain fluency requires much practice, drill, review, and frequent use so that reading becomes effortless -- so effortless that we might call this ability a "phonetic reflex."

Blumenfeld's Phonics for Success makes full use of all of these proven techniques of learning. Moreover, it teaches in a logical, systematic way facts about our alphabetic system, which are usually taught rather haphazardly if at all. And it makes these facts operating knowledge for the student who wishes to learn to spell accurately and enlarge his vocabulary.

No one denies that the English alphabetic system is somewhat complex (26 letters must accommodate 44 sounds). But its complexity is hardly an excuse for not teaching it.

For far too long, teachers of reading have avoided the difficulties of our alphabetic system by teaching sight vocabularies, whole-word configurations, context clues, and incidental phonetic clues. While such methods may produce some initial success on the primary level, they are, in the long run, injurious because they violate the basic nature of our writing system and are not in harmony with its principles. They do not provide the student with a fundamental understanding of the symbolic system we use in reading and writing, an understanding that he or she must have in order to become truly literate.

It was Dr. Samuel T. Orton, the world's foremost expert on dyslexia, who first warned educators that the look-say, whole-word method could be harmful. He wrote in the *Journal of Educational Psychology* in 1929 that the whole-word method "may not only prevent the acquisition of academic education by children of average capacity but may also give rise to far-reaching damage to their emotional life."

Blumenfeld's Phonics for Success was created to make it unnecessary for any teacher to expose a child to teaching methods that can be harmful.

OUR ALPHABETIC SYSTEM

The English alphabetic system may be complex, but it can be taught and it should be taught. We have an alphabetic system of great range and flexibility. Our spellings reveal much about the history and development of our language, and once the eccentricities of the system are learned, they are learned. They do not change. The reward for learning this system is to have for one's personal use and enrichment the entire body of our published literature. Such a literary treasure is indeed the priceless inheritance of everyone who can read.

Our English alphabetic system is complex for a variety of reasons: (1) it uses 26 letters to stand for 44 sounds; (2) it uses five vowel letters to stand for at least 20 vowel sounds; (3) many consonant letters stand for more than one sound; (4) some sounds, particularly the long vowels, have more than one spelling; (5) the invasions of foreign languages have enriched English but complicated its spellings; (6) pronunciations have changed over the centuries but the spellings have not, creating many irregularities.

Despite all of this, our system is more than 80 percent consistent or regular, with most of the irregularities consisting of variant vowel spellings.

In developing this instruction program, we have taken all of the above into account. Therefore, we start out by teaching the student the short vowels, which are the most regular in spelling, in conjunction with the consonants. Then we teach the consonant blends – final blends first, then the initial blends. Last, we teach the long vowels in their great variety of spelling forms.

Thus, we proceed from the simple to the complex in easy stages, giving the student plenty of practice and drill along the way. By teaching the letter sounds in their spelling families, the student learns to read and spell in an orderly, systematic, logical way, as well as to pronounce the language with greater accuracy.

To some teachers and tutors, this will seem like an overly academic way to teach reading. And it is, on purpose, because we want the student to learn to enjoy using his mind.

In teaching someone to read English, we must decide what should come first: learning the alphabetic system or enjoying inane stories with lots of irregular sight words. The latter may seem to be much more fun for teacher and student; but does it accomplish what we want to accomplish? If our goal is high literacy, it does not.

We know from experience that the student will derive much deeper satisfaction by learning the alphabetic system first, because it will give him or her a much greater overall reading mastery in a shorter period of time.

Competency and skill are the two most important ingredients of self-confidence, and self-confidence is the cornerstone of self-esteem. Learning to read is the student's first real exposure to formal education, and a positive attitude can be instilled in the young mind by how we approach the subject at hand.

It is obvious that one learns faster and better when the knowledge one is expected to acquire is organized in such a way as to make its acquisition as easy as possible. This is the concept behind *Blumenfeld's Phonics for Success*. Our aim is to provide the student with the kind of basic knowledge that will become the solid foundation of all his or her future academic work.

While we have organized this course in a certain order to make sure that what should be learned is learned, we have also done this to make the teaching of reading as easy for you as possible.

TEACHING THE ALPHABET

For a younger child who has not yet learned the alphabet, the fastest and most efficient way to teach it is to have the child repeat it after you in alphabetical order while you point to the letters. Thus the child learns the alphabet both orally and visually. Usually the oral learning will be faster than the visual; since the oral alphabet, when repeated often enough, is learned almost like a melody or a poem. The alphabet lends itself easily to this kind of learning since it can be broken up into rhythmical and rhyming lines as follows:

```
     A   B   C   D              a   b   c   d
       E   F   G                  e   f   g
       H   I   J   K              h   i   j   k
     L   M   N   O   P          l   m   n   o   p
         Q   R   S                  q   r   s
         T   U   V                  t   u   v
             W                          w
         X   Y   Z                  x   y   z
```

<u>Capital Letters</u>
(Also known as upper case letters)

<u>Small Letters</u>
(Also known as lower case letters)

It will take some time before the child's visual learning catches up with his oral knowledge. Indeed, some children learn to recite the alphabet perfectly long before they are able to identify all of the letters at random. This is perfectly normal since the child has had much oral practice learning to speak the language. However, now he is required to do highly precise visual learning, which may take some getting used to, especially if the child has had little exposure to print.

Children with photographic memories will learn visually much faster than those not so favorably endowed. The slowest learners will be those with weak visual memories. These children will benefit most from simple alphabetic exercises, such as repeating the letters at random, several at a time, as in the Prereading Alphabet Exercises in the Workbook, and by reviewing alphabet flashcards.

Both oral and visual learning of the alphabet should be accompanied by kinesthetic learning, that is, by having the student draw the letters in both capital and lower-case forms. Drawing the letters will help the student learn their different shapes more thoroughly. A lined notebook or writing tablet should be used by the student for doing this work.

Another effective way for the child to learn to identify letters at random is to ask him or her to pick out specific letters from advertisement print matter in newspapers and magazines. In this way the student learns to recognize the letters in different sizes and type faces. This is also a good way to check on the child's vision.

Pictures are not necessary in teaching the alphabet if you do it in the systematic manner prescribed in this program. The picture the child should be looking at is the letter itself, not an apple, or a bumblebee, or an elephant.

Pictures are a distraction that can only delay learning the alphabet directly as a set of graphic symbols. We make this point because shortly after the letters are learned, the student will be taught to identify them with speech sounds, and this is very crucial.

A letter is a symbol of a sound. It is not the symbol of anything else. The letter is supposed to stimulate the mouth, lips, and tongue to make particular sounds. It is not supposed to make the student think of an apple or an elephant. He must convert groups of letters into speech, and the student will be able to do this more readily the better he associates the letters with sounds.

A word of caution: When a student is having uncommon difficulty learning or mastering any phase of the instruction, do not become impatient and do not scold. Analyze and try to pinpoint the cause of the difficulty. You may simply have to take more time than you thought necessary. Some students take a year to master what others can master in a month. Remember, the goal is not to win a race but to teach a person to read -- no matter how much time it takes to do the job well.

TEACHING THE LETTER SOUNDS

Assuming the student has learned the alphabet, we are now ready to teach the letter sounds. The student's knowledge of the alphabet does not have to be letter perfect before we move on to this next phase, for the simple reason that the student will learn the letters better as they are used.

When you are ready to teach the letter sounds, you might explain to the student something about how and why the alphabet was invented. Older students are usually quite fascinated to learn that the entire English language is made up of only 44 irreducible speech sounds. Try if possible, to appeal to the learner's intellectual curiosity. You never know what kind of a response you will get.

Students are very sensitive about their ability to learn. This is particularly true of remedial students whose self-esteem has been badly battered by failure. A learning block, or handicap, is not a reflection of basic intelligence. We all know of highly intelligent people who have trouble doing simple addition. We also know that many so-called dyslexics are very bright and have an excellent vocabulary. Therefore, always appeal to a student's basic intelligence.

When teaching younger students the letter sounds you might simply say: "Now we are going to learn the sounds the letters stand for so that you can put the letters to work for you. Each letter stands for a different sound. You will be able to read words by knowing the sounds the letters stand for."

The essence of what you want to convey to the student is that letters have meaning – they stand for sounds – and that the letters in a written word tell the reader how to say it.

In teaching the letter sounds, it is important to convey the idea that the distinct sounds of our language can be isolated and represented by written symbols. Obviously the alphabet was invented by someone who spoke clearly and heard clearly and could distinguish between the fine differences of speech sounds, between the **t** and the **d**, between **s** and **z, m** and **n,** short **a** and short **e**. But a student's attunement to speech sounds may not be very sharp. In fact, some students may articulate very poorly and require a good deal of work to improve their pronunciations. Therefore, spend as much time as is needed to sharpen your student's attunement to the isolated, irreducible speech sounds of our language as you teach the letter sounds. Be sure to pronounce all words clearly.

The alphabet is a tremendously exciting invention based on a great discovery: that all of human language is composed of a small number of irreducible speech sounds. In teaching the alphabet, you can convey to your student the excitement of this great discovery and the marvelous invention based on it. "Did you know that every word you speak can be put down on paper?" you tell the student. That's exciting. "And that's what you are going to learn to do -- to put down on paper every sound of speech you make."

Thus, you've established the concept of a set of written symbols representing speech sounds. This is the association you want to establish in the student's mind: that letters on paper stand for sounds he can make with his voice, and that the sounds he makes can be put down on paper by way of letters representing them.

Some Practical Suggestions

Please note that this manual is written as if addressed to an instructor who has one student. However, the information in this manual applies equally to a teacher who has a classroom of students.

Ideally, each student should have his or her own copy of *Blumenfeld's Phonics for Success,* plus a lined notebook in which to write the words being learned. This will reduce the need for time-consuming board work by the teacher.

Writing the words in cursive helps in learning to spell them correctly. Also, it is advisable to assign some written homework after each learning session. The purpose of homework is to speed up the acquisition, retention, and improvement of skills.

ISOLATING THE LETTER SOUNDS

In articulating or pronouncing the letter sounds, the best way to isolate a consonant sound is to listen to what it sounds like at the end of a word and repeat it in isolation.

This can be done with consonants **b**, **ck**, **d**, **f**, **g** (as in **tag** and **large**), **k**, **l**, **m**, **n**, **p**, **r**, **s**, **t**, **v (ve)**, **x**, **z (ze)**, **sh**, **ch**, **th**. Consonant **c** stands for the **k** sound before vowels **a**, **o**, and **u**; it stands for the **s** sound before vowels **e** and **i**. The letter **q** is always followed by **u** and is pronounced as if it were **kw**.

By pronouncing the isolated sounds as purely as possible, the student will be able to understand what we mean by an irreducible speech sound.

SUGGESTIONS ON WRITING INSTRUCTION

Writing is an important part of learning to read. But how should you teach the learner to write? The learner should draw the letters of the alphabet when learning the letters in isolation. But once **words** are being read, the learner should be taught to write them in **cursive script**.

Cursive helps a child learn to read. With the prevalent ball-and-stick method, it is very easy for the learner to confuse ***b*'s** and ***d*'s**. But with cursive, a ***b*** starts like an ***l,*** as in lead, and a ***d*** starts like an ***a***. The distinction that is made in writing the letters in cursive carries over to the reading process.

In addition, in writing print script, the letters will be all over the page, sometimes written from left to right and from right to left. In cursive, where all the letters are joined, the child learns directional discipline because the letters must be joined from left to right. This helps in learning to spell, for how the letters join with one another creates habits of hand movement that automatically aid the spelling process.

Of course, the learner should also be taught to print. This can easily be done after the learner has developed a good cursive handwriting.

The Benefits of Cursive for the Left-Handed Learner

Another important benefit of **cursive first** is if the learner is left-handed. A right-handed writer tilts the paper counter-clockwise in order to give one's handwriting the proper slant. With the left-handed learner, the paper must be tilted in an extreme clockwise position so that the child can write from bottom up. If the paper is not tilted to the right, the left-handed child may want to use the hook form of writing. This usually happens when the child is taught ball-and-stick first with the paper in a straight up position.

Cursive First

The reason why the child should learn cursive first, is that learning to print first may prevent a learner from developing a good cursive handwriting. However, if you learn to write cursive first, you can always learn to print later very nicely. In other words, learning cursive first does not prevent the development of a good printing style, while print first will create fixed writing habits that will prevent the development of a good cursive script.

The Little First Readers

The eleven little Alpha-Phonics Readers were created by the author of *Phonics for Success* to give the beginning student the experience of reading a book as early as the completion of Lesson 14 in the program. Children become quite elated at being able to actually read a book at that early stage of learning to read. A set of these readers can be obtained from Chalcedon Store, an Internet website. We highly recommend them as an additional learning tool for this program.

ORDER OF LESSONS

Lessons 1 – 14 teach all of the consonants with just one vowel – **short a.**

After completion of the 14 lessons, the learner will be ready to read the **First Alpha-Phonics Reader**, which consists of only **short a** words.

After successfully reading the first book, the learner will have great incentive to keep on learning so that he or she can read **Book Two.**

There are **eleven little readers** in all, to be used throughout the *Alpha-Phonics* instruction program. They were created to give the learner a sense of increased mastery as he or she learns to read.

LESSON 1: (Short a; consonants **m, n, s, t, x**)
Have the learner turn to Lesson 1 in the Workbook. Start by telling the learner that you are now going to teach the sounds the letters stand for. Say:

> *"When you learned the alphabet, you learned the names of the letters. Now you're going to learn the sounds the letters stand for. Let's start with the first sound. Now listen to the sound I make."*

Make a **short a** sound. (The **short a** is the **a** in **at**.)

> *"Did you hear that sound?"*

Make it again and ask the learner to repeat it after you.

> *"That sound is not a word all by itself, but you hear it and say it often in many words. Can you say it again?"*

After the learner repeats the **short a** and hears you repeat it, print the letter **a** on a writing tablet.

> *"The letter **a** that you see stands for the sound you just made. It is called the **short a.** Now I am going to say five words with that sound in it, words that you use every day:* **am, an, as, at, ax.**"

Print the words in large letters on a sheet of paper or writing tablet as they appear in the Workbook. Give examples of how each word is used in a spoken sentence, so that the learner understands that they are words. Explain that a word is the smallest unit of speech that has meaning.

> "The **short a** sound all by itself doesn't mean anything. But a sound that means something is a word. **Am, an, as, at, ax** are all words because they have meaning. Now each of these words has two letters in it. Can you name the letters?"

Have the learner spell each word, saying the word after it is spelled. Spelling a word means naming its letters in proper left-to-right sequence. Ask the learner:

> "Now if each of the words has two letters and each letter stands for a sound, how many sounds does each word have?"

Repeat the word **am** slowly. Write and say the **short a** sound (**a** as in **at**); then write and say the word **am** just below it.

> "Do you hear the difference between **short a** (pronounce **a**) and **am**? When we say **am**, we add another sound to the **a**. What is the sound we added to the **a** in the word **am**?"

Say the **m** sound (**mmm**) as said in the word **am**. (To correctly isolate this consonant sound, listen to what it sounds like at the end of a word; then lift it from the rest of the word. By doing so, you will minimize injecting a vowel element.) After you've made the **m** sound, ask the learner:

> "Did you hear it? Can you say it?"

After the learner says the **m** sound, tell him or her that the letter **m** stands for the "**mmm**" sound.

> "So if we want to write the word **am**, we must write **a-m**, because these are the letters that stand for these sounds."

Repeat the procedure for **an, as, at,** and **ax**. The letter **n** stands for "**nnn**," the letter **s** stands for "**sss**." (Actually, the **s** in **as** is a soft **s**, which sounds more like "**zzz**." Just as the vowel letters represent more than one sound, some consonants also have variant sounds. But at this stage, we are teaching only the sounds used in the words presented in the Workbook.) The letter **t** stands for "**tuh**," and the letter **x** stands for "**ksss**."

Have the learner print these words, say them, and spell them. (If you wish to start teaching the learner cursive writing, this is a good place to begin.) In any case, make sure that the learner understands that each word has two sounds and that he or she can match the right sound with the right letter. Point out how the name of each consonant letter gives a hint of the sound each letter stands for. Exaggerate the sounds so that the learner can hear them distinctly and recognize them when heard.

When you are convinced that the learner knows these letter sounds thoroughly, tell them that there are two kinds of letters in the alphabet: vowels and consonants. The letter **a** is a vowel and **m, n, s, t,** and **x** are consonants. The other vowels are **e, i, o,** and **u** All the rest are consonants, although **y** is sometimes used as a vowel. Explain that the vowels are the most powerful letters in the alphabet, because you can't have a word without one. Consonants need vowels in order to make words. In English, consonants rarely, if ever, stand alone. You needn't elaborate at this point. We merely want to establish the fact that there are two classes of letters: vowels and consonants.

By now the learner has learned a great deal. He or she is beginning to hear words with a greater awareness of their different sounds, and the learner has seen how these different sounds are represented in the Workbook by alphabet letters. The learner sees that the letters are printed from left to right in the same sequence as they are spoken. The five words can also be printed on cards and flashed to the learner in short drills to help develop quick recognition.

LESSON 2: (Initial consonants **S, m, h, s, t**)

Usually, you can proceed into Lesson 2 in the same tutoring session as Lesson 1. However, if there is a break between the lessons, do a quick review of Lesson 1 before proceeding into Lesson 2.

Now, have the learner turn to Lesson 2. Point to the word **am**. Then point to the letter **S** in front of it. Explain that he or she has been introduced to a new word and ask the learner if he or she can figure it out by sounding it out. The word is the name **Sam**. Ask the learner how many sounds are in that word. Then ask the learner to articulate the three sounds in the order they are printed (**SSS-aaa-mmm**). Explain that we use a capital **S** at the beginning of the word, **Sam**, because it is a proper name and all proper names begin with a capital letter.

Repeat the procedure with **an**. Explain that the letter **m** placed in front of **an** makes the word "**man**" (**mmm-aaa-nnn**). Then have the learner articulate the three sounds.

Then point to the next word, **as**. Introduce the new letter, **h**. Articulate the sound of **h** as "**huh**." Explain that the **h** put in front of **as** makes the word **has**. Then, ask the learner if he or she can figure out the next two words (**sat** and **tax**) by sounding them out. Again, have the learner write these words. Tell the learner to be sure to sound the words out as he or she writes them. Remember, writing the words will help learners reinforce what they are learning.

LESSON 3: (Review words; first sentences)
All of the words learned in Lessons 1 and 2 have now been arranged in their spelling families. Have the learner read them. Explain to the learner that he or she now knows enough words to be able to read and write two simple sentences: **Sam sat** and **Sam has an ax**. Explain that a sentence always begins with a capital letter, whether or not the first word is a name, and that it ends with a period. Tell the learner that a sentence is a complete thought and that the period at the end of the sentence is called **punctuation**. For practice, have the learner write a page or two of the words and sentences in Lesson 3.

LESSON 4: (Consonants **d, D, w**)
Introduce the letter **d** and its sound, "**duh**." Show how we can make the word, **ad**, by placing the letter **a** in front of the letter **d**. Expand **ad** into **dad** by simply placing the letter **d** in front **ad**. Introduce the letter **w** and its sound, "**wuh**." Place the letter **w** in front of the word **ax** and see if the learner can sound out the word, **wax**. Then, place a capital **D** in front of the letter **an** to make the name **Dan**.

Have the learner read the two new sentences. Show the learner how to write capital **D** and **W**, and lower case letters **d** and **w**. Again, have the learner write a page or two of the four new words and the two sentences in this lesson.

You may want to proceed directly into the next lesson if the learner is making quick progress. It is up to you to decide how far to proceed in one session. The lessons can vary from 15 minutes to one-and-a-half hours, depending on the age of the learner and his or her attention span. Always allow enough time for writing practice. If you are a tutor, and are only tutoring the learner once or twice a week, enough homework should be given so that what is learned is retained from session to session.

LESSON 5: (Alphabetic word building)
By now the learner should begin to understand the principle behind alphabetic word building, how each letter's sound is used in writing words. Have the learner read the words downward in each spelling family column.

Introduce under **ad** the new words **had, sad, Tad,** and **mad**. Explain that these words are made by placing the letters already learned, **h, s, t,** and **m**, in front of the word **ad** to make these new words, just as was done with the word **dad** in Lesson 4. Point out that the word **Tad** begins with a capital letter because it is a proper name.

In the second spelling family column, introduce the new words **ham** and **dam**, again by placing the letters **h** and **d** in front of the word **am**. Explain the meaning of **dam**. In the third column, introduce the word **tan**.

In the fourth column, introduce the new word **was**. Point out that **was**, while in the **as, has** spelling family, is pronounced **"wuz."** This is an irregular pronunciation. Thus the learner will have been made aware that there are inconsistencies in our phonetic system. In the case of **was**, the learner will have no problem remembering the correct pronunciation since **w-a-s**, if pronounced as the other words in its spelling family, would be meaningless. There is no word in English pronounced "waaaz" (rhyming with **has**) and that is why a child will have little difficulty learning the irregular pronunciations since the spoken language is their guide to correct pronunciation.

In the fifth column, introduce the words **hat** and **mat**. And in the sixth column, introduce the name **Max**.

Also show how these same words have been arranged in alphabetical order in the bottom half of the lesson. Discuss how alphabetical order is used -- in dictionaries, telephone books, in listing towns on maps, in listing book titles and authors in libraries -- which is to help us find what we are looking for more easily.

In five short lessons, the reading vocabulary of the learner has now been expanded to 25 words.

LESSON 6: (**Short a** sentences, punctuation)
All of the sentences in Lesson 6 are made up of words the learner has already learned. Have the learner read the sentences. Explain that we place a question mark at the end of a sentence that asks a question. Once the learner is able to read the sentences with ease, have him or her write them on the writing tablet or in a notebook.

LESSON 7: (Consonant blend **nd**; initial consonant **l**)
Add **d** to the end of **an** to make the word **and**. Explain that **nd** is a blend of two consonant sounds, **nnn** and **duh** ("**nnn-duh**"), and make sure the learner can hear and identify the three sounds in the word **and**. Ask the learner if he or she can hear the difference between **an** and **and**. Show how **and** is used.

Point to the letters **h, l,** and **s**, and explain that by placing these letters in front of the word **and** you now have the words **hand, land**, and **sand.** Introduce the sound of the initial consonant l ("lll") in making **land**. For practice, have the learner write the letter l in capital and lower case form.

Have the learner read the sentence, **"Dan and dad had land and sand."** Then have the learner read the next four lines and capitalize the names -- **Dan** and **Sam, Max** and **Tad** -- when writing them.

LESSON 8: (Consonants b, c, g, f, j, l, n)
Introduce l as a final consonant, and the capital **A,** as in the name **Al**. Have the learner add the capital letters, **H** and **S**, to **al** to form the names **Hal** and **Sal**.

As done previously, introduce the other consonant letters in this lesson. Have the learner read the list of words under each of the consonants presented. Introduce the letter **Bb** in both capital and lower case forms; then have the learner read the new words: **bad**, **ban**, **band**, and **bat**.

Introduce the letter **Cc**, which stands for the **"kuh"** sound, as in the word **cat**. Later, the learner will learn that **c** also stands for the **"sss"** sound when it appears before the letters **e** and **i**. But for the moment, simply teach the letter **c** as standing for the **k** sound. Have the learner read the list of words under the letter **Cc**. Be sure that the learner recognizes the capital **C** in the name **Cal**.

Introduce the letter **Gg**. It stands for the **"guh"** sound as in **gas**. Later, the learner will see that **g** can also stand for the soft **"juh"** sound, as in **gem**.

Introduce **Ff** as standing for **"fff,"** as in the word fan. Introduce the letter **Jj** as standing for **"juh,"** as in the word **jam**. Introduce initial **Ll**, as in the word **lab**. Introduce initial **Nn** as in **nab**. As the learner is introduced to each new letter, have him or her read the words in each column.

Be sure to have the learner practice writing the words in these lessons as they are introduced.

LESSON 9: (Consonants p, r, t, v, w, y, z; final consonant k)
Introduce consonants **Pp, Rr, Tt, Vv, Ww, Yy** and **Zz** as initial consonants, and explain that the letter **p** is also used as a final consonant in this lesson. Articulate the sounds as follows: **p** as pronounced **"puh"** in the word **pal**; **r** as **"rrr"** in the word **"run"**, review **t** as in **tab**, **v** as **"vuh"** in the word **van**, review **w** as in **wax**, **y** as **"yuh"** in the word **yam**, and **z** as **"zzz"** in **zag**. Introduce the

learner to final consonant **k** sound as in **yak**. (The word **yak** is shown as the first word under the initial consonant **y**.) Make sure that the learner can articulate each irreducible consonant sound. Have the learner read all of the new words and discuss the meanings of those he or she may not know.

LESSON 10: (Review of **short a** words)
This is a review of all the words learned thus far, with a few more new words added. The words are arranged in their spelling families. Have the learner read the words down each column to test the learner's knowledge of the sounds of the consonant letters. Correct all errors in reading. Have the learner spend as much time as necessary to develop proficient knowledge of these consonants. Have the learner spell and sound out words he or she finds difficult to read.

LESSON 11: (Consonant digraph **ck; qu**)
Introduce the consonant digraph **ck** as standing for the **k** sound. A consonant digraph is a single consonant sound represented by two consonant letters. Although the word **back** has four letters, there are only three sounds in the word (**b-a-ck**). Have the learner read the words in the lesson. Also, introduce the **qu** spelling form, as in the word **quack**. Note that **qu** has the same sound as **kw**. Have the learner write these words for practice.

LESSON 12: (**a** as a word)
Introduce the word **a**, as in **a cat**, **a hat**, etc. Like the word **an**, it is an indefinite article meaning "one."

LESSON 13: (Sentences)
Have the learner read the sentences and write them for practice. Writing the words and sentences will help the student learn correct spelling.

LESSON 14: (Review of **short a** words and syllables)
In this lesson, we have drill columns consisting of words and nonsense syllables comprised of the consonants learned thus far in combination with **short a**. Many of the nonsense syllables will later turn up in multisyllabic words. A syllable, incidentally, is a unit of speech with at least one vowel sound.

Have the learner read down each column. If the learner is having difficulty with any word or syllable, have him or her spell it and then sound it out. Also, on page 19, introduce the initial consonant **k** in the column with **kab, kac, kack**, etc.

The purpose of this drill is to help the learner develop a phonetic reflex, that is, the automatic ability to associate letters with sounds. The columns can also be read across.

After completing Lesson 14, the learner should be given Book 1 of the First Readers to read.

LESSON 15: (Short a, e, i, o, u)
Introduce the rest of the short vowels: **e, i, o,** and **u.** Have the learner pronounce the five short vowels in isolation: **short a** as in **bad, short e** as in **bed, short i** as in **bid, short o** as in **Bob,** and **short u** as in **bud**.

Have the learner read across the columns in order to be able to hear the contrasting short-vowel sounds. The aim of this lesson is to get the learner to associate the right vowel sound with the right vowel letter.

LESSON 16: (Short e)
Have the learner expand his or her reading vocabulary by learning all of the **short e** words in this lesson. Discuss the meanings of words the learner may not know.

Explain that the letter **c** stands for the **k** sound before vowels **a, o,** and **u,** but stands for the **s** sound before vowel letter **e,** as in the word **cell,** and before letters **i** and **y.** Note that the letter **g** most often stands for the **"juh"** sound before vowels **e, i,** and **y,** as in **gem, gin,** and **gym**.

Have the learner write these words for spelling practice.

LESSON 17: (Short e sentences)
The sentences in this lesson incorporate many of the newly learned **short e** words. Have the learner read the sentences and write them. Have the learner read the sentences aloud so that the parent or tutor can get a sense of the learner's progress. Also, a benefit of having the learner write the sentences is so that he or she can become accustomed to writing complete thoughts with correct spelling, grammar, and punctuation.

LESSON 18: (Short e words and syllables)
In this lesson we do with **short e** what was done with **short a** in Lesson 14. Have the learner read the nonsense syllables and words in their columns and at random. Explain to the learner that many of the nonsense syllables will later turn up in multisyllabic words, such as **level, lesson, never, velvet,** etc.

Note that initial consonant **c** should be pronounced as **s** in this exercise, and pronounced as **k** in the final position.

LESSON 19: (Short **i** words; **f** as **ph**)
Expand the learner's reading vocabulary to include the **short i** words in this lesson. Introduce **ph** as another spelling of the **f** sound, as in the name **Phil**. Also see if the learner can read the two-syllable name: **Philip**.

LESSON 20: (Short **i** sentences)
Have the learner read the sentences in this lesson and write them for practice. Teach the learner the use of the comma, as shown in two of the sentences. Commas help us phrase the sentences correctly, so that they can be read fluently, with the proper pauses and inflections. There is a rhythm to speech, and punctuation helps us see that rhythm in print.

LESSON 21: (Consonant digraph **th**)
Introduce the consonant digraph **th,** which stands for the **"thuh"** sound. Articulate the sound and have the learner repeat it. Ask the learner if he or she can hear the **th** sound in such words as: **the, them, this, that, bath, Beth**, and **with**.

A consonant digraph is not a blend. We simply do not have enough letters in our alphabet to stand for all of our separate sounds, so we sometimes use two letters to stand for one irreducible sound. This is the case with **th**. Just as there is a hard **s** and a soft **s**, there is also a hard **th** as in **thin,** and a soft **th** as in **the**. Have the learner read the list of words and make sure the he or she pronounces each word correctly. The learner shouldn't have any trouble pronouncing the proper **th** sound since the spoken word is the key to how the written word is pronounced.

LESSON 22: (Sentences with **th** words)
Have the learner read the sentences in this lesson, which incorporate the newly learned **th** words. Have the learner also write the sentences.

LESSON 23: (Short o)
Here we concentrate on **short o** words. Have the learner articulate the **short o** in isolation and then read the words in the columns. Note that the words **son, ton**, and **won** vary in pronunciation from the rest of the words in their spelling family. Note that the words **off** and **dog** are pronounced differently in various parts of the country. Learners should say the words as they are generally said in their region.

LESSON 24: (**Short o** sentences)
The sentences in this lesson incorporate the newly learned **short o** words. Have the learner read them and practice writing them.

LESSON 25: (Plural **s**, **es**, and possessive **' s**)
Introduce the learner to the use of **s** and **es** to designate plurals and the **apostrophe s** (**' s**) to designate possession or ownership, as in **Don's hat**. Have the learner read the words in this lesson and write them for practice.

LESSON 26: (Sentences with **s**, **es**, and **' s**)
The sentences in this lesson incorporate what was learned in Lesson 25. Have the learner read the sentences and write them for practice.

LESSON 27: (**Short u**)
In this lesson, we concentrate on the **short u**. Have the learner articulate the **short u** in isolation, and then read down the columns of words. Note the irregular pronunciations of **full**, **bull**, **pull**, and **put**. By pointing out the irregular words, we affirm the consistency of everything else. Again, the spoken word is the proper guide to pronunciation.

LESSON 28: (**Short u** sentences)
Have the learner read the sentences and write them for practice. Make sure that the irregular words are pronounced as they are normally spoken.

LESSON 28a: (Consonants **b** and **d**)
If the learner often confuses **b** and **d**, use these drill columns for practice.

After completing Lesson 28a, the learner should be able to read Book 2 of the First Readers.

LESSON 29: (Consonant digraph **sh**)
Introduce the consonant digraph, **s-h**, which stands for the "**sh**" sound, as in **ash** and **shag**. This is another single consonant sound represented by two consonant letters. Have the learner read the words and practice writing them. The words **bush**, **push**, and **wash** vary in vowel pronunciation from the other words in their spelling families. Again, the spoken language is the proper guide to pronunciation.

LESSON 30: (Consonant digraph **ch**)
Introduce the consonant digraph **c-h**, which stands for the "**ch**" sound, as in **chap** and **rich**. Expand the learner's reading vocabulary to include the words in this lesson. Have the learner write them for practice.

LESSON 31: (Consonant digraph **wh**)
Introduce consonant digraph **w-h**. It's pronounced as if it were spelled **h-w-u**, "**hwuh.**" Articulate it carefully to distinguish it from simple **w**, "**wuh.**" Generally there is not much detectable difference in common speech between **wh** and **w**. However, it is important for the learner to know how to spell the **wh** words correctly. Note that **what** does not rhyme with **cat** but rhymes more with **nut** or **not**, depending on the local pronunciation. Have the learner read the words and write them for practice.

LESSON 32: (Review of **sh**, **ch**, **wh** words)
This lesson consists of a review of short-vowel words with the consonant digraphs learned in the previous lessons. Have the learner read the words. Pay close attention to the proper pronunciation by the learner.

LESSON 33: (Sentences with consonant digraphs)
The sentences in this lesson include all of the consonant digraphs learned thus far. Have the learner read the sentences and write them for spelling practice.

LESSON 34: (Verbs **to be** and **to have**)
At this point introduce our two most common verbs, **have** and **be**, and their tenses. The learner is already familiar with the words **am**, **is**, **was**, **has**, **had**. The words **have**, **are**, **they**, **were**, **you** are common but irregular words. The learner already knows the sounds of their consonant letters, so teach these words as sight words. The sole purpose of this lesson is merely to expand the learner's ability to read more interesting sentences. However, these words will be more thoroughly studied when encountered later in their own spelling families.

LESSON 35: (Sentences)
This lesson consists of practice sentences using the words learned in Lesson 34. Have the learner read the sentences and write them for practice. You may want to read the sentences aloud to the learner and have the learner write them as you dictate them, and thereby test spelling.

LESSON 36: (Contractions)
Introduce contractions; that is, two words contracted into one. For example: **is not** is contracted into **isn't**, **can not** into **can't**, **has not** into **hasn't**, **it is** into **it's**, **let us** into **let's**, and **did not** into **didn't**. Note that an apostrophe is used to indicate where the two words are contracted. Have the learner read the words and write them for practice.

LESSON 37: (Sentences with contractions)
Have the learner practice the sentences in this lesson. Point out that the apostrophe, when used in a contraction, denotes where a letter has been left out. In the word **Peg's**, the apostrophe signifies possession.

After completing Lesson 37, the learner should be able to read Book 3 of the First Readers.

LESSON 38: (Two-syllable, short vowel words)
In this lesson, we introduce the learner to many two-syllable words composed of simple short-vowel syllables. Again, a syllable is a unit of speech with only one vowel sound in it. It can have one or more consonant sounds, but only one vowel sound. Have the learner read the words first divided into syllables, then as whole words. For example: **hot-dog, hotdog – box-top, boxtop – zig-zag, zigzag – cat-nip, catnip**; and so on. This will convey to the learner the phonetic structure of multisyllabic words and how they can be read by recognizing their syllabic units.

With practice this process becomes so automatic that we can read most multisyllabic words with instant recognition. It is only when we encounter difficult multisyllabic words, like the many new medical terms, that we have to stop and break up the word into syllables in order to read it correctly. Once we pronounce the word correctly several times, it can be read easily.

This lesson is also a good time to test spelling. After the learner has become familiar with the words, give him or her a spelling test. The results will tell you how well the learner has learned the alphabetic principle. If you detect any weaknesses, go back to previous lessons for additional practice.

LESSON 39: (Sentences with two-syllable, short-vowel words)
Have the learner read the practice sentences in this lesson, which include many of the two-syllable words learned in Lesson 38.

After completing Lesson 39, the learner should be able to read Book 4 of the First Readers.

LESSON 40: (a as in **all**; sentences)
Introduce the sound of **a** as the "**au**" sound in **all, call** and **fall**, and other double l words in this spelling family. Explain that the letter **a** stands for more than one sound. The learner already knows the **short a** sound, as in **Al, Cal,** and **pal**; but when two l's (**ll**) follow the **a**, we get **all, call, pall**, etc. Have the

learner read the words and the sentences in this lesson and write them for spelling practice.

LESSON 41: (Consonant blend **ng**; **ing** words)
We introduce the **ng** consonant blend, which is found at the end of such words as **sing, rang,** and **long.** Explain that a blend is bringing two consonant sounds closely together so that they blend. In this case, you can hear the **n** blending with the **g.**

Expand the learner's reading vocabulary with the **ng** words in this lesson. Have the learner read across the columns so that he or she will hear the contrasting short vowel sounds as **ang, ing, ong, ung.** For practice, have the learner write the words.

In Lesson 41, introduce the name **Washington** as shown divided into three syllables. First, ask the learner if he or she can decode the word without help by simply sounding out the syllables and putting them together.

Have the learner read down the columns. Note that the final consonant of most short vowel syllables is doubled when adding **ing.** Have the learner write the words for spelling practice.

LESSON 42: (Sentences with **ing** words)
Have the learner read the sentences in this lesson and practice writing them.

LESSON 43: (Final consonant blends **nd**, **nt**)
In this lesson we review the final consonant blend **nd** and introduce the final consonant blend **nt**. Note that the pronunciations of **want** and **wand** are slightly different from the other words in their spelling families. The letter **w** seems to alter the sound of **short a** whenever it precedes it.

LESSON 44: (Sentences with **nd** and **nt** words)
Have the learner read the sentences in this lesson and write them to practice spelling.

LESSON 45: (Final syllable **er**; **er** words and sentences)
Introduce the syllable **er**, which is really a variant **r** sound. (The **e** in **er** is also considered a distinct variant vowel sound, but it is too minor to be taught as such.) Show how by adding **er** to many already known words, the learner can expand his or her reading vocabulary to include many new words. Have the learner read the short practice sentences and make up others, and write them for spelling practice.

LESSON 46: (Final consonant blends **nk**, **nc**, **nch**)
Introduce the learner to final consonant blends **nk** as in **tank**, **sink**, and **junk**; **nc** as in **zinc**; and **nch** as in **ranch**, **inch**, and **lunch**. Note that **nch** is made up of a consonant digraph plus a consonant. Expand the learner's reading vocabulary to include the words in this lesson. Have the learner write the words for practice.

LESSON 47: (Sentences with **nk**, **nc**, and **nch** words)
Have the learner read the sentences in this lesson, which include the final consonant blends just learned.

LESSON 48: (Final consonant blends **ct**, **ft**, **pt**, **xt**; sentences)
Introduce final consonant blends: **ct** as in **act**, **ft** as in **aft**, **pt** as in **apt**, and **xt** as in **next**. Have the learner read the words and sentences. Some of the words may be new to the learner. Discuss them and use them in appropriate sentences to demonstrate their meanings. Have the learner write these words to practice spelling.

LESSON 49: (Final consonant blends **sk**, **sp**, **st**; sentences)
Introduce final consonant blends: **sk** as in **ask**; **sp** as in **gasp**; **st** as in **best**. Have the learner read the words and discuss those that are new. Have the learner write the words and sentences for spelling practice.

After completing Lesson 49, the learner should be able to read Book 5 of the First Readers.

LESSON 50: (Final consonant blends **lb**, **ld**, **lf**, **lk**)
Introduce final consonant blends: **lb** as in **bulb**, **ld** as in **held**, **lf** as in **elf**, and **lk** as in **milk**. The words **bald**, **calf**, **half**, **talk**, and **walk** are irregular in their pronunciations. The **a** is pronounced "**au**" in the word **bald**, and the letter **l** is silent in the words **calf**, **half**, **talk**, and **walk**. Since there are no other words in English that can be represented by these spellings, the learner should have no trouble reading and spelling them. Have the learner read the words and of course write them for practice.

LESSON 51: (Final consonant blends **lm**, **lp**, **lt**)
Introduce final consonant blends: **lm** as in **elm**, **lp** as in **help**, and **lt** as in **belt**. Note that the words **halt**, **malt**, and **salt** are also irregular words. As in the word **bald** in the previous lesson, the letter **a** is pronounced "**au**" in these three words. Have the learner read the words in this lesson and write them for practice.

LESSON 52:   (Final consonant blend **mp**)
Introduce final consonant blend **mp** as in **camp**. Have the learner read the words and write them for practice.

LESSON 53:   (Final consonant blend **tch**; sentences)
Introduce final consonant blend **tch** as in **catch**. The **tch** blend is really a spelling variant of consonant digraph **ch**. **Rich** rhymes with **itch**, and **much** rhymes with **hutch**.   Rhyming helps learners remember these words and spellings more easily.

Have the learner read and write the words in this lesson and learn the meanings of new words. Explain that there are many variant spellings of the same sounds in English. That's what makes our alphabetic system so rich and flexible. Just as **k** and **ck** stand for the same sound, so do **ch** and **tch** at the ends of words. Explain that **ch** sometimes also stands for the **k** sound. We shall take that up in a later lesson. Have the learner read the practice sentences. Note the irregular pronunciation of **a** in **watch**.

LESSON 54:   (Final consonant blend **dge** and **nge**)
Introduce final consonant blends **dge** as in **badge** and **nge** as in **tinge**. Have the learner read the words and sentences and write them for practice.

LESSON 55:   (Final consonant blends **nce**, **nse**)
Introduce final consonant blends **nce** as in **dance** and **nse** as in **rinse**. Have the learner read the words and sentences and write them. Note that **once** rhymes with **dunce**.

LESSON 56:   (Review of words with final consonant blends)
All of the final consonant blends learned in Lessons 41 through 55 are reviewed in this lesson. Have the learner read and write the words.

LESSON 57:   (Two-syllable words with consonant blends)
Many two-syllable words are made up of simple, short-vowel words and syllables combined with other short-vowel words and syllables. In this lesson, many of these words and syllables have consonant blends and digraphs. For example: **contest**, **sandwich**, **selfish**, etc. Have the learner try to decode these words on the basis of what they have learned thus far. This is a good way to find out how well the learner has progressed and to determine if the learner needs additional practice and drill.

LESSON 58: (Initial consonant blends **bl, br**)
Introduce initial consonant blends **bl** as in **blab** and **br** as in **Brad**. Expand the learner's reading vocabulary to include the words in this lesson. Discuss the words that are new to the learner, using them in appropriate sentences to demonstrate their meaning. Have the learner write the words for practice. Make up practice sentences if desired.

LESSON 59: (Initial consonant blends **cl, cr**)
Introduce initial consonant blends **cl** as in **cliff** and **cr** as in **crab**. Expand the learner's reading vocabulary to include the words in this lesson. Have the learner write the words for practice. Make up practice sentences if desired.

LESSON 60: (Initial consonant blends **dr, dw**)
Introduce initial consonant blends **dr** as in **draft** and **dw** as in **dwell**. Expand the learner's reading vocabulary to include the words in this lesson. Have the learner write the words for practice. Make up practice sentences if desired.

LESSON 61: (Initial consonant blends **fl, fr**)
Introduce initial consonant blends **fl** as in **flat** and **fr** as in **frog**. Expand the learner's reading vocabulary to include the words in this lesson. Have the learner write the words for practice. Make up practice sentences if desired.

LESSON 62: (Initial consonant blends **gl, gr, gw**)
Introduce initial consonant blends **gl** as in **glad**, **gr** as in **grab**, and **gw** as in **Gwen**. Expand the learner's reading vocabulary to include the words in this lesson. Have the learner write the words for practice. Make up practice sentences if desired.

LESSON 63: (Initial consonant blends **pl, pr**)
Introduce initial consonant blends **pl** as in **plan** and **pr** as in **press**. Expand the learner's reading vocabulary to include the words in this lesson. Have the learner write the words for practice. Make up practice sentences if desired.

LESSON 64: (Initial consonant blend **sl**)
Introduce initial consonant blend **sl** as in **sled**. Expand the learner's reading vocabulary to include the words in this lesson. Have the learner write the words for practice. Make up practice sentences if desired.

LESSON 65: (Initial consonant blends **shr, sm, sn**)
Introduce initial consonant blends **shr** as in **shred**, **sm** as in **smell**, and **sn** as in **snap**. Expand the learner's reading vocabulary to include the words in this lesson. Note that **shr** is made up of a consonant digraph and a consonant.

Have the learner write the words for practice. Make up practice sentences if desired.

LESSON 66: (Initial consonant blends **sp**, **spl**, **spr**)
Introduce initial consonant blends **sp** as in **spell**, **spl** as in **splash**, and **spr** as in **spring**. Note that **spl** and **spr** are blends of three consonant sounds. Expand the learner's reading vocabulary to include the words in this lesson. Have the learner write the words for practice. Make up practice sentences if desired.

LESSON 67: (Initial consonant blends **st**, **str**)
Introduce initial consonant blends **st** as in **stick** and **str** as in **strand**. Note that **str** is a blend of three consonant sounds. Expand the learner's reading vocabulary to include the words in this lesson. Have the learner write the words for practice. Make up practice sentences if desired.

LESSON 68: (Initial consonant blends **sw**, **sc**, **sk**, **scr**)
Introduce initial consonant blends **sw** as in **swim**, **sc** as in **scan**, **sk** as in **skip**, and **scr** as in **scrub**. Note that **scr** is a blend of three consonant sounds. Note the irregular pronunciation of the words **swan** and **swamp**. (The **a** in these two words are pronounced as "**ah**.") Expand the learner's reading vocabulary to include the words in this lesson. Have the learner write the words for practice. Make up practice sentences if desired.

LESSON 69: (Initial consonant blends **tr**, **thr**, **tw**)
Introduce initial consonant blends **tr** as in **trim**, **thr** as in **thrill**, **tw** as in **twin**. Note that **thr** is made up of a consonant digraph and a consonant. Expand the learner's reading vocabulary to include the words in this lesson. Have the learner write the words for practice. Make up practice sentences if desired.

LESSON 70: (Words with consonant blends)
This is a review of all of the consonant blends learned thus far. They are all short-vowel words, unless otherwise noted as irregular within the lesson in which they were presented. Have the learner read them and write them for practice.

LESSON 71: (Sentences)
The sentences in this lesson contain only those words and sounds learned thus far. Have the learner read them aloud so that you can evaluate his or her progress. If you detect any weak spots, go back to previous drills for reinforcement. However, move as rapidly as you can into the next series of lessons, which take up the long vowels.

After completing Lesson 71, the learner should be able to read Book 6 of the First Readers.

LESSON 72: (Long a)

Explain to the learner that he or she has learned all of the short vowel sounds and how to read them, plus all of the consonants and consonant blends. Now the student is going to learn the long vowel sounds. Explain that the long vowel sounds are pronounced the same as their letter names: **a, e, i, o, u**. That will make it easy for the learner to read such words as **be, bee, we, no, so,** etc.

We start with **long a**. Ask the learner if he or she can hear the difference between the words **at** and **ate**. On Lesson 72, point to the words and have the learner follow along with you. Explain that the silent **e** changes the **short a** to a **long a**. Explain that both words have only two sounds each, but that the word **ate** has three letters, one of which seems to be silent. Explain that it is not really silent, however, because both the **a** and the **e** separated by a consonant (**a/consonant/e**) stand for the **long a** sound. Now under the word **at** point to the words **hat, fat, mat, rat**. Under the word **ate** point to the words **hate, fate, mate, rate**. Ask the learner to explain what happened when you added an **e** to the words under **at**.

Next, point to the words **Al** and **ale**. Ask the learner if he or she can read these words. If the learners have heard of ginger ale, they will be familiar with the word **ale**. Under **Al** point to **pal, Sal, gal**, and under **ale** point to **pale, sale, gale**. Ask the learner to read these words.

The words in this lesson are arranged as described above. Have the learners read the rest of the words in the two columns, comparing sounds and spellings.

LESSON 73: (Long a as a-e)

Expand the learner's reading vocabulary to include these **long a** words. Explain that in **age** the **g** is soft as opposed to the hard **g** in **get** and **gal**. Note the three irregular words and their particular spelling families: **ache, are, have**. Explain that the **ch** in **ache** stands for the **k** sound; **are** rhymes with **car**; **have** rhymes with **lav**. Seeing these irregularities in the context of their spelling families, the learner should conclude that irregularities are few and that they tend to affirm the consistency of everything else.

LESSON 74: (Sentences with long a words)

Practice sentences with **long a** words as spelled **a/consonant/e**.

LESSON 75: (**Long a** as **ai**)
Explain to the learner that there is more than one way to write **long a**. The second most common way is **ai**. Teach these **ai** words in their spelling families. Note irregular words **said, again,** and **against. Said** rhymes with **red. Again** rhymes with **Ben**. The **ai** in **against** is pronounced the same as the **ai** in **again**.

LESSON 76: (**Long a** sentences)
Practice sentences with **long a** words. Please note the use of quotation marks in some of the sentences. Quotation marks are used when directly quoting a speaker.

LESSON 77: (**Long a** as **ay** and **ey**)
Explain that there is a third and fourth way in which **long a** is spelled. Teach the **ay** and **ey** words. Note that the **long a** in these spelling forms occurs at the ends of words. Also note that the **ey** words represent a small minority of this group and that they are really irregulars.

LESSON 78: (**Long a** sentences)
Practice sentences with **long a** as **ay** and **ey** spellings.

LESSON 79: (**Long a** as **ei** and **eigh**; sentences)
Introduce these two additional ways of writing **long a**. They are less common than **a/consonant/e, ai, ay** and **ey**, but they include some frequently used words. Expand the learner's reading vocabulary to include these words. Their use is demonstrated in the practice sentences. Point out, incidentally, that we know three ways to write **long a** (**ey, ei, eigh**) in which the letter **a** does not even appear. Note the variant pronunciation of **height**.

LESSON 80: (Review of words with **long a** spellings)
Review of **long a** words in their spelling varieties. Explain that these spellings are permanent and that simply because there are six ways to write **long a,** it doesn't mean we can spell words any way we like. We must always use the spelling that is correct.

LESSON 81: (**Long a** homonyms)
There are many words (homonyms) that sound alike but have different spellings and meanings. This is true of many **long a** words, and we can see why it is useful to have more than one way to write **long a**. It helps us identify the meaning of the word by knowing its spelling. For example, **ate** and **eight** sound exactly alike, but their spellings are so distinctly different that we know which meaning to apply immediately on sight.

Have the student learn the words in this lesson. However, do not expect him or her to learn them well at this point. The student will learn them much better after seeing them in the context of a sentence or paragraph in future reading. The purpose of this lesson is mainly to make the learner aware that such a phenomenon exists and that variant spellings of the same sound are therefore quite useful.

LESSON 82: (Two-syllable words with **long a** syllables)
See how many words the learner can figure out or decode. This is a good way to test the learner's knowledge and progress and to see where additional review and practice drills may be necessary. Make up practice sentences with these words if desired.

LESSON 83: (Vowel spellings **au, aw**)
Introduce the **"aw"** vowel sound as spelled **au** and **aw**. Teach the words in this lesson. Note irregular **aunt**.

LESSON 84: (Sentences with **au, aw** words)
Practice sentences with **au, aw** words. Make up additional sentences if desired.

LESSON 85: (a as in **ma, car**)
Introduce the sound of **a** (**"ah"**) as in **ma** and **car**. This is the fourth sound of **a** we have learned. The first three were **short a**, **long a**, and **a** as in **all**. Expand the learner's reading vocabulary to include the words in this lesson. Note the slight **a** sound variation with the irregular words.

LESSON 86: (Sentences with **a** as **"ah"** words)
Practice sentences with **a** as in **ma** and **car**.

After completing Lesson 86, the learner should be able to read Book 7 of the First Readers.

LESSON 87: (Long e as ee)
Introduce the **long e** sound in its most common spelling form **ee**. Expand the learner's reading vocabulary by teaching the **ee** words in their spelling families. Explain that the **kn** in **knee** and **kneel** stands for the **n** sound, that **been** rhymes with **in**, and that **be, he, me, we** and **she** are all long **e** words.

LESSON 88: (Long e sentences)
Have the learner read the **ee** sentences and write them for spelling practice.

LESSON 89: (**Long e** as **ea**)
The second most common way of writing **long e** is **ea**. Expand the learner's reading vocabulary to include the words in this lesson. Note the variety of irregular words in the **ea** group. In **sweat, threat, sweater, dead, head, lead, read, bread, breath, deaf,** and **meant** the **ea** is pronounced as a **short e**. **Bear, pear, tear, wear,** and **swear** all rhyme with **air**. **Realm** and **dealt** have a **short e** variation as in **melt**. **Steak** and **break** rhyme with **cake**. **Great** rhymes with **ate**. Note that **tear** as in **teardrop** and **tear** meaning **rip** can only be read correctly in context. The same is also true of **read** (present tense) and **read** (past tense).

LESSION 90: (**Long e** sentences)
Practice sentences with **ea** words. Have the learner write them.

LESSON 91: (**Long e** as **e-e**; sentences)
Long e is also spelled **e/consonant/e** as in the words in this lesson. Note the exceptions: **there, where, were, eye. Eye** is one of the most irregular words in our written language. However, even in this case, the **y** suggests a **long i**. The distinctive spelling of the word makes it easy to learn and distinguish from its homonyms. Have the learner read the practice sentences.

LESSON 92: (**Long e** as **ie**; sentences)
Long e is also spelled **ie** as in the words in this lesson. Note the exceptions, **friend** and **receive. Friend** rhymes with **blend**, and **receive** reminds us of the rule "**i** before **e** except after **c**." Have the learner read the practice sentences.

LESSON 93: (**Long e** as **y**)
This particular spelling form is usually found at the end of words as shown in the lesson. Note these irregular pronunciations: **pretty** rhymes with **city; busy** rhymes with **dizzy; money** rhymes with **sunny; any** and **many** rhyme with **penny; key** rhymes with **me**.

LESSON 94: (**Long e** as **y** sentences)
Practice sentences with **long e** as **y**. Have the learner write them.

LESSON 95: (Plural **ies**)
Teach the learner that when a word ending in **long e** as **y** is made plural, the correct spelling is **ies**. With verbs ending in **y**, we also apply the **ies** spelling change; for example, "I study often," "He stud<u>ies</u> often." Have the learner study the words in this lesson. Make up practice sentences.

LESSON 96: (Review of **long e** words)

Review of **long e** words in variant **long e** spellings.

LESSON 97: (**Long e** sentences)
Practice sentences with **long e** words. Have the learner write them.

LESSON 98: (**Long i** as **I, y, ie,** and **uy**; sentences)
Introduce the **long i** sound and its several variant spellings: **y, ie,** and **uy**. Teach the learner these variant spellings. Introduce the letter **I** as a word. Have the learner read the sentences and write them for spelling practice.

LESSON 99: (**Long i** as **i-e**; sentences)
Introduce the **long i** spelling form **i/consonant/e**. Have the learner read all of the spelling families in this lesson. Note the irregular words **isle** and **aisle**, **give** and **live**, and **knife**. Have the learner read and write the practice sentences.

LESSON 100: (**Long i** as **igh**; sentences)
We find this archaic spelling in some of our most common words. Expand the learner's reading vocabulary to include the words in this lesson. Also, have the learner read the practice sentences and write them.

After completing Lesson 100, the learner should be able to read Book 8 of the First Readers.

LESSON 101: (Spelling forms **ough** and **augh**)
Introduce the archaic spelling forms **ough** and **augh**, representing the "**au**" sound, by teaching the common words in this lesson. Note the irregular pronunciation of **though** ("**tho**"). These words are generally easy to learn because of their distinctive spelling. Have the learner read the practice sentences, make up others, and write them.

LESSON 102: (**f** as **gh**)
Introduce **gh** as another way the **f** sound is spelled. Expand the learner's reading vocabulary to include the words in this lesson. Note that the **ou** in **rough** and **tough** is pronounced as **short u**; the **au** in **laugh** is pronounced as **short a**. Have the learner read the practice sentences and write them.

LESSON 103: (**Long o** as **o e**)
Introduce the **long o** sound. The most common spelling for **long o** is **o/consonant/e**. Expand the learner's reading vocabulary to include the words in this lesson. Point out the irregular words in their particular spelling families: **soul, come, some, one, once, none, done, gone, lose, whose, move, prove,**

dove, **love**, **glove**, and **shove**. Note that in column 5 **close** is listed twice. The first is pronounced as in "close the door." The second is pronounced as in "stand close to the door."

LESSON 104: (**Long o** sentences)
Practice sentences with **long o** words spelled with **o/consonant/e**. Have the learner write them.

LESSON 105: (**Long o** as **oa**; sentences)
Expand the learner's reading vocabulary to include the words in this lesson. Note irregular words **broad, source, court**, and **course**. Have the learner read and write the practice sentences.

LESSON 106: (**Long o** as **ow**; sentences)
This is the third way **long o** is spelled. Expand the learner's reading vocabulary to include the words in this lesson. Note irregular words **owe, dough,** and **though**. Have the learner read and write the practice sentences.

LESSON 107: (**Long o** as in **old**; sentences)
Expand the learner's reading vocabulary to include the words in this lesson. Note the irregular words **cost** and **lost**. Have the learner read and write the practice sentences.

LESSON 108: (Common irregular words)
It is best to teach these words in the context of the practice sentences. Explain that **to, too,** and **two** all sound alike but have different meanings. **Too** is regular, while **to** and **two** are not. **Do, who,** and **you** rhyme with **too; youth** rhymes with **tooth; young** rhymes with **sung**. Have the learner write the sentences for spelling practice.

LESSON 109: (**oo** as in **good food**)
Introduce the two sounds of **oo** as in **good food**. Expand the learner's reading vocabulary to include the words in this lesson. Note irregular words: **boor, poor, moor** rime with **lure; door** and **floor** rhyme with **more**; and **flood** and **blood** rhyme with **mud**. Note also the irregular spelling of **soup** and **group**.

LESSON 110: (Sentences with **oo** words)
Have the learner read and write the sentences with **oo** words.

LESSON 111: (Spelling form **ould**; sentences)

Introduce the archaic spelling **ould** which sounds like **"ood"** in **wood**. Expand the learner's reading vocabulary to include these common words and their contractions. Have the learner read and write the practice sentences.

LESSON 112: (**ow** and **ou** as in **cow** and **ouch**)
Introduce **ow** and **ou** as in **cow** and **ouch**. Explain that **ow** stands not only for **long o** in one set of words (see Lesson 106), but also stands for the **ow** sound as in **cow** in another large set of words. Most of these words are quite common, and therefore the learner will have little trouble determining which sound applies. The irregulars in this group are **touch, doubt, rough, tough, enough, wound** (injure), **youth, four, pour, tour, your, fourth**, and **mourn**.

LESSON 113: (Sentences with **ow, ou** words)
Have the learner read and write the sentences in this lesson.

LESSON 114: (**oy** as in **boy**; **oi** as in **oil**; sentences)
Introduce the **oy, oi** sound as in **boy** and **oil**. Expand the learner's reading vocabulary to include the words in this lesson. See if he or she can figure out or decode the two-syllable words. Have the learner read the practice sentences, make up more if desired, and write them.

LESSON 115: (**Long u** as **u-e**; sentences)
Introduce the **long u** sound and its most common spelling form, **u/consonant/e**. Give examples by pronouncing such words as **use, June, cube, mule**. Expand the learner's reading vocabulary with the words in this lesson. Note the **sh** pronunciation of **s** in **sure**. Have the learner read and write the practice sentences.

LESSON 116: (**Long u** as **ue** and **ui**; sentences)
The **long u** is also spelled **ue** and **ui**. Expand the learner's reading vocabulary with these **ue, ui** words. Have the learner read and write the practice sentences.

LESSON 117: (**Long u** as **ew** and **eu**; sentences)
The **long u** is also spelled **ew** and **eu**. Expand the learner's reading vocabulary with the words in this lesson. Note the irregular pronunciation of **sew** which rhymes with **grow**. Also note the irregular **through**. Have the learner read and write the practice sentences.

After completing Lesson 117, the learner should be able to read Book 9 of the First Readers.

LESSON 118: (er, ir, or, ur, ear; sentences)
The **"er"** sound group has a variety of spellings: **er, ir, or, ur, ear**. Note the general interchangeability of spellings in this sound group. The correct spellings, however, are best learned in spelling families. Have the learner read and write the practice sentences. Also have the learner decode the two-syllable words.

LESSON 119: (Words ending in **le**; words with silent **t**; sentences)
Many common two-syllable words in English have an **le** ending in which the **l** sound terminates the word. Expand the learner's reading vocabulary with the words in this lesson. Note the silent **t** in **hustle, bustle**, and **rustle**. Also have the learner read and write the practice sentences.

LESSON 120: (Additional **f** as **ph** words)
The learner has already been introduced to **ph** as representing the **"f"** sound. This lesson has additional words for the learner to become familiar with.

LESSON 121: (**"sh"** as **ti, ssi, ci, ce, sci, xi, su, ssu**;
  "zh" as **si, su**; and **"ch"** as **tu, ti**; sentences)
These words are of Latin derivation, but their pronunciations have been anglicized. Note **zh** as a separate and distinct consonant sound, like the French **"je,"** without its own spelling form in English. Have the learner read and write all of the words and sentences in this lesson and note the correct spellings.

LESSON 122: (Additional **n** as **kn** words)
The learner has already been introduced to several words in which the **kn** represents the **n** sound, as in **knee**. Familiarize the learner with the other **kn** words in this lesson.

LESSON 123: (**m** as **mb**; **t** as **bt**)
There is a spelling group in which **mb** stands for the **m** sound. Expand the learner's reading vocabulary with the words in this lesson. Also note that **bt** is pronounced as **t** in **debt** and **doubt**. The **b** in these words is silent.

LESSON 124: (Silent **h**)
There probably was a time when the **h** in these words was pronounced. But now it is not. Familiarize the learner with these words. In the **gh** words, teach **gh** as representing the **g** sound as in **go**.

LESSON 125: (**r** as **wr**)
Introduce consonant digraph **wr** as representing the **r** sound. Expand the learner's reading vocabulary with the **wr** words in this lesson.

LESSON 126: (s as st; f as ft)

Introduce **st** as representing the **s** sound and **ft** as representing the **f** sound, as in **wrestle, often,** and the other words in this lesson. Expand the learner's vocabulary to include these new words.

LESSON 127: (k as ch; s as ps)

Introduce **ch** as a variant spelling of the **k** sound as shown in this group of words. Introduce **ps** as representing the **s** sound, as in **psyche.**

LESSON 128: (y as short i)

Introduce **y** as **short i** as in the words in this lesson. Most of these words are of Greek origin.

After completing Lesson 128, the learner should be able to read Book 10 of the First Readers. Book 11 contains poems and songs for the enjoyment of the learner.

What Comes After *Phonics for Success?*

With the completion of the final lesson, the learner is now ready to start reading any suitable outside literature. Some learners will require continued review of the alphabetic system in order to achieve reading and spelling mastery. Learners should read and write as much as possible in order to hone their academic skills.

English literature, vocabulary development, grammar, composition, are what come next after learning to read. Achieving high literary requires learning everything that will make a student a master of his or her own language. Children, of course, teach themselves to speak their own language virtually from birth without the help of certified teachers. That's a remarkable learning achievement. But that self-taught vocabulary is limited and can only be expanded by reading great authors and their masterpieces.

As for classroom reading, it is recommended the teacher use a variety of good poetry, fiction and nonfiction texts that will stimulate the learner's appetite for the printed word. Libraries offer the young reader a tremendous variety of books on all subjects.

Children particularly enjoy reading such popular adventure and mystery series as the Hardy Boys, Nancy Drew and the Henty books. These books create a voracious reading appetite and set a healthy pattern for life-long pleasure reading.

At this point it is important to get learners into the habit of using the dictionary to look up the words they do not understand. That is the only way to increase one's reading and speaking vocabulary. Too many learners retard their own intellectual growth by never bothering to look up the words they don't understand. The student must learn that there is no shortcut to vocabulary development, without which true literacy is impossible to achieve.

Incidentally, never assume that a learner knows the meaning of a word merely because he can read it. When in doubt, ask the learner to define it.

Be on the lookout for good reading material for your learners. Once the learner realizes how much of real value can be found in the written word, reading will become an important part of that individual's life.